THE STORY OF
CATHOLICS IN AMERICA

The Story of Catholics in America

Edited by

Don Brophy
and
Edythe Westenhaver

PAULIST PRESS
New York/Ramsey/Toronto

Library of Congress
Catalog Card Number: 77-14811

ISBN: 0-8091-2087-9

Published by Paulist Press
Editorial Office: 1865 Broadway, New York, N.Y. 10023
Business Office: 545 Island Road, Ramsey, N.J. 07446

Printed and bound in the
United States of America

Contents

Introduction

This book is a concise overview of the history of the Catholic Church in the United States from pre-colonial times to the present day. As much as possible we have tried to make it the story of the Catholic people rather than the story of the institution, even though institutional figures stand out in it. Throughout the book we have stressed ways in which the American experience and the Catholic experience have come together, sometimes to clash and sometimes to strengthen each other.

Most American Catholics know very little about the history of their own national Church. It is likely that the graduate of a Catholic college or university has never heard of John Carroll, James Gibbons, Isaac Hecker, or John Hughes. Perhaps because they believed their catechisms preserved the totality of truth, Catholics of an earlier generation did not feel it was necessary to examine the twisting path that brought them to where they stood. Happily, that situation has begun to change. Through the influence of people like John Tracy Ellis and David J. O'Brien on the Catholic side and Sydney E. Ahlstrom and Martin E. Marty on the Protestant side, a new generation of Americans has begun to look at their religious roots with curiosity and sophistication.

This book is designed to serve as an introduction to American Catholic history for readers with little prior knowledge of the subject. The format, and in many cases the actual text, is based upon a filmstrip entitled *Catholics/Americans* that was produced by Paulist Press in 1975. The heartening response to the filmstrip encouraged the publication of the present volume. Where this book is being used as a classroom text, teachers may want to use the filmstrip in conjunction with the written material. The sections of the audio-visual correspond exactly to the sections of the book.

The filmstrip and the book that followed it were really the work of many people, not all of whom can be acknowledged here. However, special recognition should be given to Gerald P. Fogarty, S.J., George Fitzgerald, C.S.P., Patrick J. Riley, R. Emmett Curran, S.J., James B. Sheerin, C.S.P., and David J. O'Brien who prepared the original scripts for the filmstrip.

*Eusébio Kino, left, an early Jesuit missionary to the South-
west, was also a rancher, an explorer, and a mapmaker.
Isaac Jogues, right, lost several fingers when he was tor-
tured by the Indians. He was later killed by the Iroquois.*

*An early view of the Mission of San Luis Rey, one of the
nearly two dozen mission stations established by the Franciscans along the Pacific coast.*

I
Founding Fathers

1. The New Land

Before any people came to America, the land existed. It was a land of almost unimaginable wealth in natural resources, brimming with forests and wide, verdant prairies. There were rivers that nourished the soil and served as highways for the first Indians who came across the land-bridge from Asia or by sea from Africa. There were no cities then. There were no roads, no cars, no apartment houses, no factories, no stores, no suburbs, no crowds of people, no churches. There was only the land, standing untouched—seven and one-half million square miles of land in North America alone.

The first settlers, the Indians, were as awed by the vast size of the American continent as the Europeans who came later would be. The Indians built their religion around the majesty and power of nature, praying to the Father who directed the changing seasons, and the Mother Earth who continually brought forth new life and nurtured it. Their religion gave them a place in what they felt was a conscious design in nature.

The first European settlers set foot in this land with a sense of awe that is hard for us to understand today. Its sheer size, its potential wealth, its simple purity, appealed to them tremendously. To them it seemed to be like the Garden of Eden—with a pot of gold in it instead of an apple tree.

Unfortunately, the lure of wealth—whether it be in gold, or furs, or farmland for settling—cast an evil spell on the more mercenary Europeans. They enslaved the Indians or murdered them by the thousands without feeling any moral qualms. It was argued that the Indians were not human beings anyway.

However, with the first explorers came the missionaries, and it is with them that the history of the Catholic Church in America begins. From the start the missionaries who accompanied the first expeditions sought to protect the Indians and to convert them. At last they convinced the pope in Rome to issue a decree stating that the Indians possessed human souls and deserved respect.

The story of the Catholic Church in this new land can be told from the point of view of the Spanish, French, or English settlements in North America— since all of them lent color and shape to the Church that was to grow there. Let us take each of them in turn.

Spanish Settlements

As everyone knows, the first voyage of Columbus took place in 1492 under the auspices of Spain. The first Spanish settlements were centered on the Caribbean islands. Within a few years, however, those who followed him reached the North American continent. It is likely that the first Mass celebrated in what is now the United States was presided over by one of those missionaries who accompanied the Spanish to Mexico and then north to present-day Arizona or California.

One religious ceremony that is amply documented is the one celebrated on the coast of Florida when the Spanish landed there on the Feast of St. Augustine in 1565. The colony they founded was named, naturally, St. Augustine, and remains so to this day. It saw the establishment of the nation's oldest parish, with records dating back to 1594.

As with most places, that colony had a difficult time getting started. Indian opposition was fierce, and for the missionary martyrdom was a real possibility.

Florida remained in Spanish hands until the year 1821 when it became a part of the United States. The greatest Spanish contributions, however, took place farther west in Mexico and southwestern United States. There the Spanish *Conquistadores* came riding their terrible horses (the Indians had never seen horses before) and looking for gold. There was little gold to be found, especially on the American side of the Rio Grande, and so the soldiers finally went home. But the missionaries who came with them remained.

One of the first was a Jesuit named Eusébio Kino. Kino was an unusual man: an astronomer of some note, a mapmaker, an explorer, and a rancher. Actually Kino was Italian by birth (his original name was Chino or Chini), but he came to America under Spanish auspices and served in their territories. In eleven years he made forty expeditions through

Arizona, New Mexico and California, and is credited with baptizing 4,000 Indians.

Kino's principal mission was at San Xavier Del Bac near present-day Tucson. The mission still exists. However, the church that stands there now was built after Kino's death.

Kino is remembered as the man who first established the typography of Lower California—that long peninsula, now part of Mexico, that juts southward from the American coast. Until Kino's day Lower California was thought to be an island, but the missionary's trips across the Colorado river convinced him that the land was indeed a peninsula. The map that he drew still exists.

Kino had hoped to extend his missions along the Pacific coast into California itself. He died before he could do it. The man who accomplished what Kino dreamed of was another extraordinary missionary named Junípero Serra.

Serra was 56 when he first came to California, an old man hobbled with leg ulcers. His illness made it difficult for him to ride horses, so Serra frequently walked the hundreds of miles that separated the first mission stations. Of course there were no roads at that time.

It is estimated that Serra baptized 6,000 Indians in the last years of his life. He also started nine missions which over the years grew into settlements, then towns, and sometimes into cities—places like San Diego, Santa Clara, San Luis Obispo, and San Francisco.

It is important to realize that those Franciscan missions were more than mere churches. They were places of culture. Here the Indians could come for food when they needed it, for learning, and for protection. Along with the message of faith, they were taught the principles of agriculture. Elsewhere in the New World the Church and the army shared control over the native population, a fact that didn't stop soldiers from treating the Indians harshly. In the California missions, however, Serra and his fellow priests were able to win full authority over the welfare of the local residents. Their safety was thus insured.

The history of the California missions is a sad one. Once influential centers of learning and piety, the missions fell to ruin when Mexico won its independence and expelled Spanish citizens from its soil. Other than the buildings themselves, very little remains to tell of those first missionary efforts. But the faith that was planted in the hearts of the people—both Indians and settlers—continued to smoulder until California became a United States territory and new missionaries came from the east to rebuild the churches and reopen the schools.

The French Settlements

Far away to the northeast the French were creating their own testimonials to faith, and to commerce.

The French first came to the New World looking for territory and for useful trading goods such as furs. Jacques Cartier first came to present-day Canada in 1534, although formal colonization didn't begin until almost a century later.

The French were aided immensely by the waterways of lakes and rivers that crisscrossed the northeast part of the continent. Soon explorers and missionaries were voyaging across the Great Lakes and down the Ohio and Mississippi Rivers to Louisiana. New Orleans was founded in 1718.

The first French missionaries—two Franciscans—came to stay in 1615. Father Louis Hennepin, who accompanied LaSalle's famous expedition to the upper Mississippi, was a Franciscan. Within a few years, however, the French missions were given to the exclusive jurisdiction of the Jesuits, and the missionary story henceforth would be theirs.

One of the most famous of the early missionaries was Jacques Marquette. In 1673 he accompanied the explorer Joliet on a canoe voyage from Green Bay, Wisconsin, to a point halfway down the Mississippi River. Marquette's health was ruined by the arduous journey. Nevertheless, after a short rest he set out to establish his own missionary station in the wilderness. He never made it. His health deteriorated; he died at the age of thirty-seven.

What happened to Marquette serves to underline the hazards of missionary life in those days. Men with university degrees from Europe came to America to ride in bark canoes and sleep on the bare ground. The priests and brothers had to be as good with axes as they were with sermons. They were constantly threatened by the perils of the wilderness, by sickness, and by Indians. And nowhere was this more true than in New York State.

In 1642 a Jesuit priest named Isaac Jogues was captured by the Iroquois Indians. The Hurons had been friendly to the French, but the Iroquois were their deadly enemies. Jogues was taken to an Indian village near Auriesville, N.Y. where he underwent painful tortures (losing several fingers in the process). At last he managed to escape.

Helped by Dutch Protestants, Jogues made his way from Albany to New Amsterdam (modern-day New York City—where, Jogues noted, there were only two Catholics), and finally back to Paris. It would have been easy for him to remain there, yet within a year he was on his way back to Canada to resume his missionary work.

Again Jogues headed for Iroquois country. Again he and his companions were captured. This time he did not escape. Jogues was one of eight Jesuits martyred by the Iroquois.

It might seem as if those first missionaries met with unremitting hostility from the Indian tribes, but such was not the case. In time even the Iroquois were converted. Among the converts was a teenage girl named Kateri Tekakwitha who trekked 200 miles alone from her village to live with Christians near Montreal. Her intense devotion had a profound effect on everyone who knew her.

For the most part the French treated the Indians well. They mingled with them, and sometimes even married them. When the French started a new settlement they usually lived in peace with the neighboring tribes. This was in marked contrast to the English practice of driving the Indians away and taking over their land.

The Abenaki Indians of Maine are a case in point. This tribe had been converted by French Jesuits and lived peacefully as Christians. But in 1727 an expedition of English soldiers from Massachusetts destroyed the Abenaki mission and killed its priest, Sebastian Ralé.

English Settlements

It must be admitted at the very beginning that the English, who didn't like or trust the Indians, had little affection for the French and Spanish either. Those old antagonists—Protestant England against Catholic France and Spain—carried their ancient hostilities from the Old World to the New where they continued to burn amid the green forests of North America.

Much of the future history of the Catholic Church in America will be colored by the fact that it was the English king who won control of North America and not some Catholic monarch. Yet it must also be admitted that it was in the unpromising soil of English America that the main trunk of the American Catholic Church grew, and eventually blossomed.

The first English Catholics came to America to escape persecution at the hands of Protestants back home. They owed their patronage to George Calvert who, with the title of Lord Baltimore, became a Catholic while he was secretary to King James I.

Deciding to create a refuge for his persecuted brethren, Calvert obtained a large tract of land along Chesapeake Bay. His son, Cecil Calvert completed plans for the colony and called it Maryland (after Henrietta Maria, the Catholic wife of King Charles I). In March of 1634, two small ships, the *Ark* and the *Dove*, landed on St. Mary's Island carrying 300 settlers, most of them Protestants, and three Jesuits.

While Catholics held most of the leadership positions in early Maryland, they were conscious of the fact that their political position was still very tenuous. Many of their fellow-residents were not Catholic, and the shadow of the Protestant monarch was never far away. Since they needed freedom for themselves, they would have to extend it to everyone. Therefore, in 1649 Maryland passed an Act of Toleration guaranteeing that no Christian should be compelled to worship against his or her consent. (It should be noted that the Act does not include Jews, who were very few in number.) This act provided four decades of peace in the new colony, until 1688 when the colonial government was arbitrarily dismissed and Anglicanism made the state religion.

Then followed many years of trials for Maryland Catholics. The capital was moved from St. Mary's to Annapolis. The old statehouse was burned. In 1704 penal laws were passed against Catholics. They could hold no office. They could have no churches. Public worship was forbidden to them; Catholics came secretly to "mass houses" for their services.

Through all of this the Catholics endured, and survived. Here and there in the colonies they reached positions of importance. In New York, for example, an Irishman named Thomas Dongan served as governor and permitted religious toleration; but he too was ousted after five years.

Many Catholics found refuge in Pennsylvania where freedom of worship was protected by William Penn's Quakers. St. Joseph's Church, the first in Philadelphia, was opened in 1734. For a time it was the only Catholic church legally open for public worship in the whole British Empire.

Despite their best intentions, even the Quakers couldn't help being a little suspicious about their "popish" neighbors. On one occasion they mistook a Corpus Christi procession for a military drill. And in

1757 during the French and Indian War the Pennsylvania assembly passed a law forbidding Catholics to use or possess firearms.

All things considered, Catholics in the American colonies probably suffered less persecution than did their brothers and cousins in England. There was so much room in North America, and there were so few people, that the issues which seemed so important to Europeans generated less friction here. This fact enabled the Catholic Church to grow, very slowly at first, but grow.

2. Days of Revolution

By the year 1775 the American colonies were ripe for revolution. The long-simmering dispute between the king and his American subjects had reached a point of no return.

For a brief period during the previous generation a border war had united the English and colonists against a common enemy—the French. But that war was finished now. Quebec had been captured. Canada had fallen, and British rule was firmly established in the eastern half of North America.

What King George III could not command was the loyalty of his American subjects. His determination to tax them and his heavy-handed interference in the operation of colonial governments met with mounting opposition.

One of the crowning blows, in the eyes of many Americans, was the passage of the Quebec Act by Parliament. This measure, meant to conciliate the newly-conquered French Canadians, promised free-

British troops marching through New York. In a formal battle Americans were no match for their opponents, but the continent was too vast for the British to subdue.

Charles Carrol of Carrollton, left, the only Catholic to sign the Declaration of Independence, was a cultured, wealthy citizen of Maryland. The Marquis de Lafayette, right, symbolized the help given to the United States by France—help which greatly softened the traditional American suspicion about Catholics.

dom of worship to Catholics there. The Protestant majority in the thirteen colonies was severely offended. In Philadelphia the First Continental Congress denounced the Quebec Act, calling it "dangerous in the extreme to the Protestant religion and the civil rights and liberties of all America." King George was accused of being a traitor to his oath to defend the Protestant religion.

The Catholics Choose a Side

As the argument between England and America reached its boiling point, the small, Catholic minority that lived in the colonies had to decide which side to support. The choice was not difficult to make. The English crown had systematically persecuted its Catholic subjects and deprived them of their rights for more than 200 years. Catholics could find no reason to run to its defense now.

The patriotism of American Catholics found a hero in Charles Carroll of Carrolton, the son of an old Maryland family and an ardent supporter of the revolution. Carroll showed his true colors in a debate with a loyalist (a supporter of the king) which was printed in the *Maryland Gazette*. His opponent tried to besmirch Carroll's reputation by pointing out that he was a Catholic—whose word, presumably, could not be trusted—but Carroll won the debate handily.

Carroll described himself as "a man of independent fortune, interested in his country, and a friend of liberty." Indeed, he was all those things. At the time of the revolution he was one of the richest men in America. His father and grandfather before him had been prominent citizens in Maryland and protectors of the Catholic population there.

As the time of revolution approached, old barriers against Catholics holding public office were falling away. Maryland chose Charles Carroll as one of its delegates to Congress. He arrived in 1776, just in time to sign the Declaration of Independence, the only Catholic to have that honor.

Granted that Catholics had chosen to support the side of liberty, still another question remained to be answered: Did the rest of the Americans want their support? Was there too much suspicion in the air to allow Protestants and Catholics to work side-by-side?

Finding answers to these questions was greatly facilitated by the character and bearing of Charles Carroll. Regarded warily when he first came to Philadelphia to sit in Congress, he soon won many allies with his friendliness and good manners.

On top of this it rapidly became evident that the independent colonies needed all the help they could get.

Suddenly alert to the realization that Catholics had longstanding grievances against the king, some people in Philadelphia began wondering if the French Catholics in Canada couldn't be persuaded to join the patriot cause. Late in 1776 a three-man delegation was sent to Quebec to investigate the possibility. Its members were Charles Carroll, Benjamin Franklin, and John Carroll, Charles's cousin who was also a priest.

The delegation failed to attract any allies. The French listened politely, but declined the invitation, remembering only too clearly the antagonism that existed between Canada and the thirteen colonies from the days of the French and Indian War. In fact the bishop of Quebec threatened to excommunicate any Catholic who went south to fight the English.

The Catholic Contribution

Since at the time of the revolution Catholics made up less than one percent of the colonies' total population, their contribution to the overall war effort was necessarily small. However, after the war John Carroll observed that the blood of Catholics "flowed as freely (in proportion to their numbers) . . . as that of any of their fellow citizens."

For instance, there was Stephen Moylan, whose brother was a bishop back in Ireland. Moylan served on Washington's staff and finished the war as a major general.

Then there was John Barry, a young sea captain from Philadelphia, who created a small fleet of ships that ferried supplies to Washington at Valley Forge. Barry is considered the "father" of the American navy.

But the most decisive help came from the Catholic kingdoms of France and Spain. Early in the war, eager to strike a blow at their ancient rival Britain, the two nations created a secret fund to buy arms and clothing for Washington's army.

As time went on and the Americans had gained some victories, France and Spain became active participants. A French army and a French fleet were sent to America where they tipped the scales at the decisive battle at Yorktown.

From all across Europe idealistic noblemen came

hurrying to support the American cause. No one stopped to consider that they were Catholic and that their adopted nation was almost entirely Protestant.

Thaddeus Kosciusko arrived from Poland to organize Washington's engineering corps. His countryman, Casimir Pulaski, was a cavalry officer who fought in several battles and was mortally wounded in the siege of Savannah.

Finally, and most important, was the Marquis de Lafayette, an indomitable commander under Washington and a beloved figure wherever he went in the new nation.

The arrival of so many people from Catholic countries had an immediate effect on the religious atmosphere in America. These new allies must not be offended by any means. Washington took pains to stop his troops from celebrating Guy Fawkes Day— that traditional anti-Catholic fete which used to culminate by burning the pope in effigy. Washington called it "a ridiculous and childish custom."

Before the French ambassador first arrived in Philadelphia, Tory newspapers warned that he was bringing a boatload of crucifixes, hairshirts, and torture instruments. But when he arrived those myths were quickly dispelled. Everyone decided that Ambassador Conrad Gerard was a charming fellow, and most members of Congress happily accepted his invitation to attend a thanksgiving Mass to mark the third anniversary of the Declaration of Independence.

Encounters such as this not only helped the war effort, they helped to eradicate centuries of misunderstanding that had been generated by religious wars in Europe. The independent United States was embracing religious liberty not only in theory but in fact. Indeed, the next few decades would prove to be a high-water mark of religious toleration in America. Not until the mid-20th century would equivalent toleration be realized.

First, however, that toleration had to be written into law. With the war ended, Catholics in the new nation were anxious to have their rights set down in writing. Two Catholics helped to draft the Constitution, Thomas Fitzsimons of Philadelphia, and Daniel Carroll (the brother of John and cousin of Charles). However they did it with some misgivings since the Constitution said nothing about freedom of worship.

When George Washington was sworn in as the first president, a committee of Catholics wrote to him, in effect asking him to support the enactment of a Bill of Rights. They said freedom was owed to them as the price of blood spilled in the revolution.

Washington wrote back with these words: "I presume that your fellow citizens will not forget the patriotic part which you took in the accomplishment of their revolution and the establishment of its government; or the important assistance they received from a nation [France] where the Roman Catholic religion is professed."

The Bill of Rights completed the work of revolution by protecting freedom of religion and other basic human rights. The American people had set themselves free. They were free not only of British rule, they were free to be whatever they wanted to be—whether Catholic, Protestant, or Jew, believer or unbeliever—without outside interference.

3. A National Church

In 1776, although Americans found themselves with a new nation, American Catholics didn't automatically have a new Church. They were still saddled with old institutional forms that pre-dated the revolution and which tended to link American Catholics to English Catholics.

Consider these facts: The Catholic Church had existed in Maryland for almost 150 years without ever having a bishop. Of course there were bishops in Mexico and Canada, but there were none in the thirteen American colonies.

The majority of Americans in those days were what we might call "low church" Protestants. They were a devout, God-fearing people but were opposed to the "trappings" of ornate "high church" Episcopalians and Catholics. Even the Anglicans didn't have a bishop in America. An Anglican bishop who attempted to land in Boston was chased back to his boat and returned to England.

In the eyes of the Catholic authorities in Rome, America was still a mission territory. (Officially, it would remain a mission territory until 1908.) All the priests in America were Jesuits, since the American missions were considered the exclusive jurisdiction of the Jesuit order.

However, just three years before the revolution, as the result of political intrigue in Europe, the Jesuit order was suppressed. That meant that the priests in America became diocesan clergy, and instead of reporting to their Jesuit superiors in Rome they were instructed to report to Bishop Richard Challoner in London. When war came the link with Bishop Challoner was broken, and the American Catholic people and clergy found themselves without anyone in charge.

America Gets a Bishop

Into the power vacuum that existed in the American Church at the time of the revolution stepped the extraordinary figure of John Carroll. As you recall, John was the cousin of Charles Carroll and was a member of that three-man delegation sent to Canada in the early days of the war.

John Carroll was the son of the respected and wealthy Maryland family we noted earlier. He was born in Upper Marlborough, Maryland in 1735 and received his early education at a small Catholic school maintained at a place called Bohemia Manor.

When he was old enough John—or Jackie as everyone called him—was sent with his cousin Charles to study in Europe. While at school in Flanders he decided to become a Jesuit priest and was ordained. For a period after that he was a teacher, first at Liège, and then at Bruges.

After the suppression of the Society of Jesus, John Carroll returned to Maryland. He refused to accept the authority of Bishop Challoner. Instead he carried on a private ministry from his home.

Those were difficult days for Carroll, for his country, and for his Church. It seemed that he and all the other people of his day were being swept along by events that were out of control. Even his trip to Canada seemed to produce little good.

Yet Carroll was using his time to write and think

about the future of the American Church. The leaders of the American revolution were talking about freedom of worship and the separation of church and state. How could these ideals be reconciled with traditional Catholic practice? Carroll began to formulate his own ideas on the problem.

Vatican officials at this time did not fully understand the mood in America. A papal representative visited Benjamin Franklin, who was then the American ambassador in Paris, offering his government the usual courtesy of suggesting a name for a new American bishop. Franklin passed the matter on to Congress which replied, in effect, that Church appointments were none of its business. One can just imagine the shock this produced in Rome. For the first time in centuries it had offered a government some say in Church affairs only to have the invitation declined.

John Carroll, for one, was angered at the way Rome handled the matter. He was becoming ever more convinced that if the new nation ought to have a bishop, its clergy should choose him. Carroll proposed that the American bishop be elected by American Catholics.

As a stopgap compromise, the Vatican appointed Carroll to serve as superior of the American mission without the rank of bishop. The task he faced was immense. His jurisdiction included all the existing states and their territories. He had few priests to help him, and very little money.

It is true, of course, that the Church in those days was small. There were only 30,000 Catholics in a population of nearly four million. Yet with the war over the Church was showing signs of growth. It was clear that a bishop with full powers was needed in

A portrait of Father John Carroll painted about the time of his trip to Quebec during the Revolutionary War. (Kennedy Galleries)

Archbishop Carroll's cathedral, still standing in Baltimore, successfully combines Greek and Byzantine influences with an American flavor.

An early view of Georgetown College, founded in 1829.

America. So with Rome's consent as many of the American priests as possible assembled in a church near Baltimore to elect their bishop.

On November 6, 1789 Pope Pius VI issued a document that formally confirmed the election of John Carroll as the first bishop of Baltimore. His diocese covered the whole United States.

Carroll was frankly delighted with the manner of his selection. He wrote to a friend, saying: "Our religious system has undergone a revolution, if possible, more extraordinary than our political one."

The time for delight, however, was short lived. The new bishop faced an immense amount of work in getting his Church organized—a reality that was complicated by vast distances, poor communications, and scant funds. One of the first needs the bishop had was for priests. He was fortunate to secure the services of French Sulpicians who had fled their own country during the French Revolution. Arriving in 1792, they established two seminaries, one located in western Maryland and the other in Baltimore. The first had problems because of its isolation, but St. Mary's Seminary in Baltimore, despite a slow start, was destined for a great future. From the doors of this school in the next few decades would come many of the leaders of the American Church.

Carroll believed firmly that it was his duty to build, in fact, an *American* Church. Like most Marylanders of his day, he felt perfectly at ease giving religious obedience to the pope while still reserving civil obedience to the secular state. Yet keeping those spheres separate did not mean that they had to be isolated from each other. Carroll felt that the Vatican should acknowledge the spirit of democracy that existed in the young American nation; if the Vatican found it awkward to do so, then he would do it. As in the case with his own election, he felt that Rome should give American Catholics a large measure of freedom to govern themselves. He also proposed that they be permitted to celebrate the liturgy in English rather than Latin—a concession that wasn't granted until the Second Vatican Council.

These matters faced by Bishop Carroll, however, were largely internal matters. The new bishop was confronted with still greater problems touching on the external relations of the Church. He was most anxious to extend and encourage the mood of good feeling that grew up between Catholic and Protestant Americans during the revolution.

He undertook this delicate task in a number of ways. First, by means of his own character, his democratic spirit, and his impeccable family connections, he reassured Protestants that they had nothing to fear from their Catholic neighbors. The doors of government and private society were open to him. When he visited Boston on a pastoral mission, for instance, Governor John Hancock insisted that the bishop stay in the governor's own home.

Next, Bishop Carroll took pains to foster the advancement of learning and culture both within his Church and in the general society. He supported the Catholic press. He helped to found the Baltimore Public Library and served many years as its president. He commissioned the building of an impressive cathedral in Baltimore designed by Benjamin Latrobe who designed the White House.

Carroll was also instrumental in the founding of Georgetown University in 1789, the first Catholic

University in the United States. In so doing, he insisted from the beginning that admission to the new college not be limited to Catholics. Noting that the University of Pennsylvania was open to students of all faiths, he made it a policy that Georgetown do the same.

Stresses Within the Church

The manner and policies of John Carroll did much to bring about a remarkable period of religious harmony in the new American republic. The persecutions and suspicions of past generations were being set aside. Catholics were beginning to be accepted as full and respected citizens of their country.

At the same time, events were underway that would eventually threaten this hard-won equality. Even in Carroll's lifetime there were signs of future problems. In 1803 the United States purchased the Louisiana Territory from France. This event, which was so beneficial to church and state at one level, presented a difficult situation to the Church. Carroll had been laboring mightily to win full assimilation for America's Catholics (who were nearly all English-speaking and of English stock) into American society. Success was within his reach. Suddenly with the acquisition of the Louisiana Territory he had to provide again for Spanish-speaking and French-speaking Catholics. Trying to fit them into Yankee America would be more difficult.

It was clear, too, that the Church was growing much too fast for one diocese to administer. Therefore, in 1808 John Carroll became an archbishop and four new dioceses were created: New York, Philadelphia, Boston, and Bardstown, Kentucky. Eleven years later, an additional four were added.

It was clear now that the young Church would need many more priests, hopefully American priests. Initial shortages were being overcome by importing clergy from Europe, but the language problems and cultural differences they brought with them were causing stress in some places.

The gravest of these stresses was the problem known as "lay trusteeism." This phrase refers to the practice, common in many Protestant churches, of incorporating the property of the church in the name of laity. (In some states it was against the law for the church itself to own property.) Carroll permitted the practice of lay trusteeism in Catholic congregations but drew the line at allowing lay people to hire or dismiss their priests.

Inevitably conflicts arose between the lay trustees and the clergy, particularly when they represented different languages and cultures. People complained that the French priests couldn't speak English well. The Irish, whose own church background was democratic and non-structured, complained that the French clergy were authoritarian. The priests retorted that the Irish were ignorant. The complaints went on and on. In some places parish meetings were the scene of fistfights. A few parishes went into schism.

The problem of lay trusteeism persisted long after Carroll's death. The first provincial council of Baltimore in 1829 at last decided to condemn lay trusteeism. After that the practice gradually died away.

Unfortunately, the action of the council also meant that lay people in the future would have less voice in

Church affairs. Control of the day-by-day workings of the Church was passing inexorably into the hands of the clergy, especially the bishops. Only Bishop John England of Charleston, South Carolina recognized that lay participation had positive value; he established a diocesan constitution whereby assemblies of laity and clergy could advise him on Church affairs.

As the years went by the American bishops amassed a large measure of control over Church operations—more control, indeed, than European bishops had. Rome, being so far away, gave the American hierarchy almost a free hand in the running of the Church. As a consequence American priests probably had less freedom than priests in Europe.

The practice of electing bishops, which was tried successfully in the case of John Carroll, never became an accepted practice in the American Church. Two hundred years later there would be groups of American Catholics clamoring for the privilege of election that was granted in Carroll's time.

Carroll died in 1815, having been a bishop for twenty-five years. He had placed a shaky, infant Church on a firm setting. His cousin Charles Carroll lived on until 1832, the last living signer of the Declaration of Independence and a greatly revered figure in the young nation.

The dream that those two men shared of a truly American Church began to fade as the 19th century brought floods of immigrants to the New Land. The Carrolls had the breeding and the charisma to bridge the gap between Catholics and Protestants. With them gone, the gap widened again. It would take a long time before Catholics and other Americans would be reconciled.

II
Growing Nation, Growing Church

4. Moving West

The "West" has always had an almost spiritual connotation for the American people. It is more than a direction. It is the lure of adventure, of possibility, of freedom and hope. Europeans who were used to the limited economic and geographical horizons of their native lands were awestruck by the spaciousness and wealth of America, and especially by the vast territories that lay west of the Appalachian Mountains.

The Revolutionary War had temporarily slowed the eastern settlers from exploiting the lands across the mountains. With the war over, they were free to turn their faces west. By 1775 Daniel Boone had already marked a trail for them through the Cumberland Gap and westward 300 miles to the Ohio River. This "Wilderness Road," as they called it, was the first of several highways for a new generation of pioneers.

According to Boone those pioneers needed only three things: "A good gun, a good horse, a good wife." He might have added good health, a good axe, and good luck.

By 1800 settlers were pouring west by the thousands. They came by foot, by horse, by wagon, or by flatboat—filling Kentucky, the Ohio valley, and the Illinois territory like so many cups. After 1825 the Erie Canal opened access to the northwestern territories, via the Great Lakes.

Naturally where the settlers went, the missionaries went too. And where the missionaries went, the Church was gradually established. Marriages were witnessed, children were baptized and educated, the dead were prayed over. With the missionaries came civilization.

The Ohio River Valley

In a land almost devoid of institutions, the missionary—whether Catholic or Protestant—was an important figure. Very often he was the glue that bound some scattered settlers into a community. Not that the missionaries settled down like the others; at first, there were too few priests for that. More likely the missionary kept on the road, visiting one settlement, then another. Months might pass before he was seen again.

What kind of men were these missionaries? Many of them were French emigrés who had set aside genteel lives in Europe to take up a frightening new kind of work in America. An ad in a Paris newspaper described what awaited them: "We offer you no salary, no recompense, no leadership, no pension, but much hard work, a poor dwelling, small consolation, many disappointments, frequent sickness, a violent or lonely death, and an unknown grave."

One man who responded to that kind of appeal was Edward Dominic Fenwick, a Dominican priest who was born in America, educated in France, and who returned to America as a missionary. He became known as "The Apostle of Ohio" as he rode on horseback from settlement to settlement, locating families who had not seen a priest for years.

Fenwick established the first Ohio church in 1818. Just thirteen years later he could count twenty-two churches, twenty-four priests, a cathedral, a seminary, and a diocesan newspaper. By then he was Bishop of Cincinnati. In the end the Paris newspaper ad was accurate. In 1832 Fenwick died of cholera, alone in a distant town, and was buried before any of his priests could reach him.

Equally important was the work of Benedict Joseph Flaget, a Frenchman who came to America expecting to teach in the seminary but who was sent out to the missions instead. Swallowing his dismay, Flaget threw himself into his work. In 1811 he became Bishop of Bardstown, the first diocese west of the Alleghenies. It was hard at the beginning—his first cathedral was a simple log cabin—but soon his work thrived. By 1815 Kentucky had 10,000 Catholics. The fine cathedral he built next at Bardstown is still standing.

Flaget started out with ten priests to help him serve a diocese that covered the present states of Kentucky, Tennessee, Ohio, Indiana, Illinois, Wisconsin, and parts of Minnesota. Few missionaries enjoyed the luxury of spending many days at home in those days. Most of their time was spent traveling.

One of his helpers was Detroit pioneer Gabriel Richard who, in addition to running a parish, found

Edward Dominic Fenwick, above left, "the Apostle of Ohio," became the first bishop of Cincinnati.

Pierre De Smet, above right, educated in France but ordained in the United States, became famous for his travels among the Plains Indians.

John Baptist Lamy, right, helped to harmonize relations between American pioneers and the old Spanish settlers of the Southwest.

time to start his own publishing house and to help found the University of Michigan. Richard was also the first priest ever to serve in Congress. He died of cholera.

Another of Flaget's priests was Simon Bruté who eventually became a bishop himself at Vincennes, Indiana. Bruté was a brilliant, eccentric Frenchman who was trained as a physician. He was a fragile man, devoted to learning, with an emaciated face, a wide smile, and a willingness to give away whatever he had. They called him "poor, crazy Bruté." He died of tuberculosis.

Life was hard for these pioneers, but progress was rapid. Indeed, so rapid was the growth of the Church in the mission territories that people back east began to talk about "Rome's plot to take over the Mississippi Valley."

In fact the condition of Catholics there was far from that of a conquering army. When someone offered to give a bed to Louis Dubourg, an early bishop of St. Louis, he answered: "My place is too small to allow for such a decorative piece of furniture. Allow me, friend, to exchange it for something more useful. Bread is what I need."

Across the Mississippi

If the frontier territories east of the Mississippi River were vast, the lands to the west of that river acquired in the Louisiana Purchase were even larger. Suddenly the western boundary of the United States was set on the Rocky Mountains.

Americans from the eastern coastal states and

from the Ohio Valley were on the move once more, across the Great Plains to Santa Fe in the southwest, or to Oregon in the northwest. Fierce Plains' Indians who were defending their traditional hunting grounds challenged the settlers every step of the way.

Missionaries frequently found themselves caught in the middle of this conflict. They felt called upon to serve the needs of the Indians as much as the needs of settlers. They also attempted to promote peace in situations where peace was the last thing either side wanted.

One of the first missionary priests to reach out to the Indians was Pierre De Smet, a young Belgian Jesuit who was ordained in Missouri. In 1840 he made his first journey among the tribes of the Great Plains. So great was his success the United States government asked him three times to serve as its representative at Indian councils.

In all De Smet traveled 250,000 miles on foot, horseback, and boat, promoting peace and starting mission stations. He was, as one army officer said, the only white man who could journey among the Plains' Indians and come out with his scalp.

However, it was not only Indians with whom the settlers, moving westward, had to content. In the southwest, where the territorial borders were unclear and not always honored, Americans began to clash with Spanish settlers—Mexicans who traced their ownership back to old Spanish land grants. Mexico protested the intrusion. In 1846 the United States and Mexico fought a brief but bloody war which at its end saw vast new areas of land added to United States ownership.

The American Catholic Church now found itself

with the care of many new citizens. These Mexican-Americans had traditions and styles of doing things that were significantly different from those of the American settlers. They had their own language, their own culture, their own loyalties, and their own churches.

This was the situation that existed when John Baptist Lamy was appointed bishop of the Territory of New Mexico. Lamy had been born and educated in France. His French background was an asset, since it helped to make him an impartial arbitrator between English-speaking and Spanish-speaking settlers.

But first, before he could bring peace to the region, he had to get there. The overland route from St. Louis along the Santa Fe trail was considered too dangerous because of Indian raids. Instead, the bishop was advised to take a ship along the Texas coast and then strike inland. He did this, but alas, the ship was wrecked and Lamy lost part of his meager possessions. At last, after a long and arduous journey, Lamy reached Santa Fe where he was to remain for the next thirty-eight years until his death.

The story of Lamy's trip to Santa Fe serves to illustrate a real fact of missionarys' lives: For them the problems of transportation and communications were far more taxing than any threat from Indians or from personality conflicts. Distance was the primary hazard. To reach the far outposts of his diocese, Lamy often had to spend weeks in the saddle, sleeping out under the stars, traversing mountains and deserts.

A half century later, Lamy's career would be the source of a novel by Willa Cather, called *Death Comes for the Archbishop*. She described the experiences of Lamy and similar men like this: "Those early missionaries threw themselves naked upon the hard heart of a country that was calculated to try the endurance of giants. They thirsted in its deserts, starved upon its rocks, climbed up and down its terrible canyons on stone-bruised feet, [and] broke long fasts by unclean and repugnant food."

In addition to these trials Lamy and the other pioneer bishops had to minister to the Indians, the English-speaking and Spanish-speaking settlers, conciliating each in turn when differences broke out among them. They had to beg for funds, build churches, and spread out a thin line of clergy to serve them.

Religious orders, too, contributed mightily to the missionary enterprise west of the Mississippi. Following in the footsteps of De Smet, Jesuit missionaries followed the earliest pioneers to Oregon and the northwest territories. Mother Duchesne's sisters provided care for Indians in the Plains region. A few years later the Oblate priests of Mary Immaculate undertook the taxing and dangerous missions along the Mexican frontier.

Life in frontier America was hard. When the missionary arrived, farmhouses were turned into churches. When they were gone, lay men and women led family prayers, taught the catechism to youngsters, and endured as well as they could.

And yet a kind of rough brotherhood was born on the frontier. The prejudices of the eastern seaboard were set aside. On the frontier, people had to cooperate in order to survive.

In this rough and cruel land it was the Church, more than most other institutions, that spread order and brought peace. It was the Church, with its learning and its sense of historical continuity, that brought stability to farms and settlements and made the process of civilization possible.

5. The Sisterhood Was Powerful

The history of the United States in the 19th century was largely the story of the American frontier. The process of pushing the frontier westward, and then settling and cultivating the land, absorbed much of the nation's energies. As we noted earlier, historians of a later generation came to regard the frontier as a symbol of American restlessness and expansionism.

In more recent years, however, historians are beginning to revise that first picture, because the United States during this period was not expanding only along its frontiers. Its population in the east was growing enormously, especially with the beginning of large-scale immigrations. Its business was booming: factories were springing up around the eastern cities, and credit was readily available. American merchant ships plied the ports of the world with goods manufactured in New England and Pennsylvania. Inventive geniuses like Eli Whitney, Samuel F. B. Morse, and Cyrus McCormack came up with new tools to make work easier and more productive.

So the east, as well as the west, was a frontier land. In the east different kinds of forces had to be tamed: bridges and canals had to be built; streams and rivers had to be dammed up to produce power. But most of all a burgeoning population had to be taught how to build the bridges and operate the machines that made the industrial revolution possible.

Education was vitally important. Many of the new immigrants didn't know how to speak English. Coming from autocratic principalities in Europe, they weren't used to participating in a democratic society. The task of forging them into a single instrument fell to the schools. And education—in a nation where every man hoped his children would do better than he—took on an almost sacred aura.

Schools in those days before the Civil War were almost as diverse as the population. They ranged from the typical one-room schoolhouse to sophisticated academies where fifth-graders learned to speak Latin. Since most schools were run by their local communities, educational standards tended to vary widely from one place to the next. In some places, like New York City, private corporations were founded to oversee the operations of "public" schools.

It hardly needs to be added that in a largely Protestant society these schools took on a decidedly sectarian flavor. It was not unusual to have a Protestant catechism used as a reading text in a public school. The history texts portrayed the Catholic Church in very unfavorable terms. In nearly all schools Protestant hymns were sung and the Bible was read—the Protestant Bible of course. And while this may not shock Catholics of today, in those days it was taken as a direct affront to their faith.

Parochial Schools Are Founded

Catholic schools go back to the earliest days of America. John Carroll attended one as a boy in 18th century Maryland. But those few schools were restricted generally to wealthier church members. It wasn't until the first immigrants arrived—to find the "public" schools in the control of hostile Protestants—that the idea of a large-scale parochial school system began to take hold.

Just as the American Church turned to Europe to find missionaries for its frontier, so it recruited priests, nuns, and brothers to serve its new schools. The Holy Cross Brothers came in 1841. The Christian Brothers came three years later. The Franciscan Brothers arrived in 1847, and the Xaverians in 1854. Notre Dame University was founded in the 1840s. A decade later Benedictine monks moved to the Minnesota farmlands and chartered St. John's University at a place now known as Collegeville.

In the long run, however, it wasn't those men who really got the Catholic school system started in America. It was the women. In fact the very first Catholic school was established by Ursuline Sisters in New Orleans as far back as 1727.

One woman more than any other was most responsible for the creation of the parochial school system that we know today. Her name was Elizabeth Ann Bayley. She was born into a wealthy New York Protestant family in 1774. Her father was a physician related to the Roosevelts.

When she was twenty years old Elizabeth married William Seton and settled into the role of a comfortable New York City wife and mother. She bore five children. But then in 1803 her husband died.

By this time Mrs. Seton was making up her mind to become a Catholic. Despite the opposition of her family and many of her friends she was baptized. But how

A Sister with her students at some unknown school in the Midwest.

A portrait, left, of Elizabeth Seton as a young woman. She bore five children before her husband died. Young Katherine Drexel, right, was the product of a wealthy Philadelphia family.

could she spend her life now as a widow cut off from the world she knew? She decided to become a teacher. Moving to Baltimore, she started a school. She was aided by other women who wanted to give their lives to the Church, and with Bishop Carroll's help they founded an order known as the Sisters of Charity.

Mother Seton was not a demure, submissive woman. She was tough and blunt, and a good organizer. Some nuns, in friendly jest, called her "Wild Betty." The sisters she recruited and trained went out from the motherhouse in Emmitsburg, Maryland to staff dozens of schools and orphanages that served the needs of immigrant Catholics.

If the career of Mother Seton set a pattern for the American Church, it was by no means unique. Several other orders of sisters were started during this period to care for poor Catholics. Ten years after Mother Seton died the Oblate Sisters of Providence were organized to care especially for Black children. Theirs was the first community of Black sisters in the nation.

Even before that the Sisters of Loretto and the Sisters of Nazareth had sprung up in frontier Kentucky. Out in the Mississippi Valley Mother Philippine Duchesne, a Sacred Heart sister, started a whole string of schools with the help of sisters who came over from France.

As the century wore on, thousands of other sisters made the long sea voyage from Europe to staff schools and hospitals that dotted the landscape of the United States. The native communities also grew. By the end of the century it was estimated that forty-five percent of the nation's 8,000 Catholic parishes were supporting their own schools. That achievement would have been impossible without the help of teaching sisters.

The Condition of Women

The accomplishments of Catholic sisterhoods in the United States was all the more remarkable when one considers the situation of women in that day. Most people would have agreed with the principle, enunciated by the English jurist Sir William Blackstone fifty years earlier, that married women had no legal existence whatsoever; all their rights and properties belonged to their husbands.

Women in the years before the Civil War were expected to be supports for their husbands, capable around the house, mildly interested in art and music, and nothing more. But there were forces at work that were beginning to change that image. Out on the frontier women were learning to farm, and ride, and shoot, and bear hardships. For them the preparation of food was a matter of survival, not luxury. In the eastern cities immigrant wives washed floors, took in piecework, and even worked in factories while still raising a family.

The combination of hard work and the first easing of social taboos was setting the stage for the first struggle for women's liberation. And for many women the Church was an outlet for their newly-discovered energies.

Philadelphia-born Cornelia Connelly was one example. Like Elizabeth Seton she was a widow with five children when she decided to become a nun and found a religious community, the Sisters of the Holy Child. Her followers taught in schools in many parts of the United States, as well as in Europe and Africa.

Another Philadelphian was Katherine Drexel who founded a community in 1891 to care for poor Blacks and Indians. Armed with great ambitions—and a family fortune to back them up—she and her Sisters of the Blessed Sacrament established more than fifty foundations in the south and southwest before her death.

And finally there was Rose Hawthorne Lathrop, the youngest daughter of Nathaniel Hawthorne, who also was married and gaining some reputation as an author before she became a Catholic and then a sister. She might have been expected to enter a teaching order of sisters, but instead she founded a community to care for people sick and dying of cancer.

Women like Rose Lathrop, Elizabeth Seton, Cornelia Connelly and others would have stood out in any cultural period. The fact that they succeeded while bound by rigid canonical rules and in a society that distrusted the very idea of convents adds to their credit. Because of the contributions of their sisters and of male religious, the American Catholic Church grew enormously in the first half of the 19th century.

6. American Nativism

When the year 1800 dawned in America, the Catholic population was no more than a tiny drop in the ocean of North America. That situation, however, was soon to change. In the first half of the century nearly one million Catholic immigrants, most of them Irish, entered the United States.

The majority of the immigrants were poor and unskilled. They found jobs building the Erie and Ohio canals. Later they worked on the railroads. Those who moved west where there was plenty of land and jobs were accepted easily. But those who settled in the eastern cities and competed for jobs were bitterly resented. Many employment agencies had signs that read: "No Irish Need Apply."

The vast majority of Americans in that day were of English Protestant stock. The English and the Irish shared a centuries-old antipathy for each other. English anti-Catholic feelings were reinforced by the memory of bitter civil wars that had disrupted their native lands for generations. And finally, in America, Protestant settlers had only to think back one lifetime to recall ugly guerilla wars fought against French Catholics in Canada.

So the seeds of religious intolerance existed in America long before the first immigrants arrived. During the Revolutionary War, when France suddenly became an ally against England, it seemed that the old hatreds might disappear. But they continued to linger. They were particularly strong in the Federalist Party and in the enclaves of Puritan New England.

The rise of Napoleon stirred up old anti-French feelings once more. The United States narrowly avoided war with France in 1799. Massachusetts-born John Adams, a Federalist, was then in the White House. Under his patronage Congress passed the Alien and Sedition Acts designed to control "foreign" elements in the United States. It was an ominous sign.

The Emergence of Nativism

The mood of suspicion and mistrust that permeated Catholic-Protestant feelings in America gave rise to a movement known as Nativism during the three decades before the Civil War. Protestant Nativists were made apprehensive by the arrival of Irish-Catholic immigrants; they wanted to see the nation preserved for the exclusive use of "native born Americans." (And by this phrase they meant themselves, not the Indians!)

The historical antagonism that separated them was heightened by economic conditions. A trade embargo during the War of 1812 all but halted shipping, making New England a depressed area. Then in 1819 the over-extension of credit caused bank panics on the east coast and in the west. Naturally, whenever there was a business slump hostility increased against immigrants and the cheap labor they represented.

Who were the Nativists? Some of them came from prominent families. No less a person than Samuel Morse (who later developed the telegraph) wrote a book warning his fellow citizens about the dangers of conspiracies plotted in Rome. Morse ran for mayor of New York on a Nativist ticket in 1836, but lost.

A Nativist firebrand in Massachusetts was Lyman Beecher, a Presbyterian minister whose daughter, Harriet Beecher Stowe, would later on be the author of *Uncle Tom's Cabin*. In August of 1834 Beecher preached three sermons that so inflamed his Boston audience that they stormed a convent of Ursuline sisters in nearby Charlestown and burned it to the ground. Fortunately, no one was killed, yet it was a sign of the violence that was to come.

The Boston mob was inflamed in part because it believed one of the Ursulines was being kept at the convent against her will. The belief was mistaken, but the rumor did not die easily. The slowness of communications in that day made it easy to start rumors and difficult to dispel them. Objective journalism was virtually unknown. The leading Nativist periodical was edited in New York by the Rev. W. C. Brownlee and modestly entitled the *American Protestant Vindicator and Defender of Civil and Religious Liberty against the Inroads of Popery*.

In such an atmosphere as this a single book or mistaken allegation could have a powerful effect on public opinion. Such a book was published in 1836. It was called *Awful Disclosures of the Hotel Dieu Nunnery in Montreal* and was written by a woman named Maria Monk who claimed to be an "escaped nun." The book abounded with stories of debauchery and murder, confirming the worst suspicions of the Nativists. As it turned out, the book was filled with so many inaccuracies and fabrications that even a blue-ribbon panel of Protestant clergymen declared it to be false. Maria turned out to be not an ex-nun but a former inmate in a Montreal institute for delinquent girls. However, that didn't stop the book from going through several printings and selling about 300,000 copies.

To combat rumors such as these, Catholics began to found newspapers and periodicals of their own. The first was the *U.S. Catholic Miscellany*, started in 1822 by the energetic Bishop John England of Charleston, South Carolina. Other cities such as Philadelphia and New York soon followed suit, establishing a pattern of diocesan newspapers that exists to this day. By the 1840s there were 20 English-language newspapers, and one in German, being published every week. In addition to presenting the Catholic position on controversial issues, the newspapers also served to unify the growing Catholic populace in those areas.

In some cases Catholic spokesmen met Nativists in public debates. Bishop England accepted the challenge of a Baptist preacher in Charleston. In Philadelphia a young priest named John J. Hughes carried on a long and acrimonious exchange with a Presbyterian minister. The debates, however, tended to settle nothing.

Nativist controversies did not dwell exclusively on lurid tales about nuns and convents. Those were only secondary matters. There was a more important issue which brought Catholics and Protestants into conflict. That issue was schools.

As we noted earlier, public education in those days was still highly flavored by the Protestant religion. School children read from the King James Bible in class and were given history books which, for instance, spoke of John Hus as a "zealous reformer from popery" who was burned at the stake by "deceitful Catholics." So distasteful was this to Catholic parents that as many as 20,000 children in New York City were kept out of the public schools, either to attend parochial schools or no school at all.

The New York City schools were then under the

control of the Public School Society which, despite its name, was not public at all. A private corporation with a strong Protestant bias, the society administered all state and city funds for public schools.

In 1840 Governor William H. Seward—a Protestant but sympathetic to the immigrants—sought to give state funds to parochial schools as well. His suggestion precipitated a bitter controversy involving himself, the Public School Society, and John Hughes, that young priest from Philadelphia who had just been made Bishop of New York. In the end the parochial schools didn't get any money, but the Public School Society was abolished and the biased textbooks were thrown out. Henceforth, public schools would be rigidly non-sectarian.

Naturally, confrontations of this kind tended to arouse passions and fears. Many Protestants were genuinely afraid that their schools would be taken over by Catholics, who were becoming the largest population bloc in the eastern cities. Those anxieties came to a head in Philadelphia in 1844 when Bishop Francis P. Kenrick politely asked if Catholic children in public schools might be allowed to read their own Bible instead of the Protestant one. Kenrick's request was misunderstood or misinterpreted. Mobs of angry citizens denounced him. Anger turned to violence. When it was over three Catholic churches and numerous homes had been destroyed. Thirteen persons were dead.

The Know-Nothing Party

Public education and issues like it inevitably

Protestant America was fearful of the growing influence of the Catholic Church. In this Thomas Nast cartoon, bishops in the form of crocodiles threaten innocent school children.

A contemporary view of the Philadelphia riots, which erupted over a disagreement about the use of the Bible in public schools.

brought politics into the ancient rivalry between Catholics and Protestants. Non-Catholics were coming to feel that political control was slipping from their hands. Immigration was increasing and the voting power of Catholics was gaining in strength.

Eventually the political opposition to Catholicism took the form of a separate political party. It was known as the American Party, or more popularly as the Know-Nothing Party since its members, who were bound to secrecy, always claimed to "know nothing" about its operations.

The Know-Nothing movement was an amalgam of secret societies, pro-slavery groups, workingmen's organizations, and militant Protestants. The one feeling they all shared was mistrust of the Catholic Church. This sense of mistrust was fueled in 1853 when a papal delegate, Archbishop Gaetano Bedini, made an ill-advised tour of several American cities. He had been sent by Rome primarily to mediate lay-trusteeism disputes, but the Nativists alleged he had come to bring the Inquisition to America. Riots and demonstrations followed him wherever he went.

In the following year the Know-Nothing Party emerged full-blown, almost by magic. Within a few months Know-Nothing fever swept the country. Violence increased. There were riots in Louisville, where six people died, and shots were fired at the cathedral in St. Louis.

In Baltimore Know-Nothing rowdies called "plug-uglies" stationed themselves outside polling places and threatened to use their "plugs" or carpenters' awls on any voter who didn't know the password. Not surprisingly, their candidate won.

The party almost won the state election in New

York. It did win, overwhelmingly, in Massachusetts where the legislature promptly created a committee to investigate the activities of convents and rectories. The so-called "sniffing committee" didn't find anything unusual and soon fell into discredit.

But that didn't stop the Know-Nothings. In 1855 Know-Nothing legislatures were elected in Rhode Island, New Hampshire, Connecticut, Maryland, and Kentucky. Several other border and southern states were almost added to the list. In addition, about 75 Know-Nothings were elected to Congress. The party confidently expected to win the presidential election of 1856.

Their expectations were not realized. As it turned out the coalition that made up the Know-Nothing movement was too fragile to endure for long. When the national convention came out in favor of slavery, its northern Protestant adherents—nearly all of whom were strongly opposed to slavery—abruptly left the movement. The Know-Nothing Party disappeared as quickly as it had emerged.

But the Nativist mentality that gave rise to the Know-Nothings has never completely disappeared from American life. Nativism is not a party. It is a feeling or fear directed against outsiders in any society. Jews suffered from it. So did Chinese and other ethnic groups. Indeed, as time went on some Catholics became Nativists themselves. Any person who claims to be "more American" than his fellow citizen is a Nativist.

However, the great organized Nativist feeling that marked the early 19th century in America did eventually dissipate. Immigrants began to feel more secure in their new homeland and contribute more to its

Know Nothings charged that the Irish (the whiskey keg) and Germans (the beer keg) were stealing municipal elections.

national life. They joined with Protestants to fight in the Civil War. They began to be accepted as full Americans.

Even at the height of the Know-Nothing movement they were moving forward. In 1853 President Franklin Pierce felt secure enough to appoint a Catholic to his cabinet. The first Catholic ever to sit in the cabinet was Roger Brooke Taney who had been named Attorney General twenty years earlier; by the time of the Civil War, Taney was Chief Justice of the Supreme Court.

There would always be some people who continued to believe that the Roman Catholic Church had designs on American freedom, but their numbers were slowly diminishing. Immigrants and other minority groups were well on their way to becoming native Americans themselves.

III
Confluence and Conflict

7. The Civil War

The United States of America waited for the 1860s like a tinder-dry prairie waits for fire. As the time approached when the struggle over slavery would be resolved, lesser rivalries were set aside. Catholics and Protestants stopped sniping at each other. Nativists and immigrants forgot to trade insults. A new drama would absorb their energies for the next decade.

The Church and Slavery

It would be wrong to view the Civil War simply as a political struggle between the north and the south. Both sides recognized from the outset that there were moral issues involved in slavery. As the current of events quickened, both sides appealed to their religious leaders to justify the moral position of their governments. In the north the early fight against slavery was led to a great extent by Protestant clergymen. Staunch New Englanders like the Beechers, so quick to assail Catholics during the Nativist controversies, were equally fierce on behalf of abolishing slavery. They believed fervently that the resulting war was a divine judgment in which God would wield his "terrible swift sword" against slaveholders.

Such attitudes inevitably created bitter divisions between northern and southern clergymen. Some denominations, like the Baptists, tore themselves apart and created separate governing structures that exist to this day.

The Catholic position on slavery was less divisive and more ambiguous. Historically the Church had permitted the existence of slavery without encouraging it. Theologians argued that slavery was permissible as long as the slaves were well cared for. By the early 19th century it was acknowledged by almost everyone that Black slaves were brutally treated when they were captured and transported from Africa, so in 1839 the Vatican condemned the slave trade. However, it was held that this condemnation did not apply to slaves already in the United States.

Slaves generally adopted the religion of their owners. At the outbreak of the Civil War it was estimated that 100,000 slaves were Catholics, more than half of them in Louisiana. Charles Carroll had owned slaves as a landholder in Maryland. So had John Carroll and some of the early Jesuits.

Catholics in the North were not as strongly opposed to slavery as their Protestant neighbors were. For one thing, immigrant Catholics tended to gravitate toward the Democratic Party, which was more conciliatory on the slavery issue than the Republican Party was. Second, the immigrants felt that those abolitionists who wept over the plight of slaves lacked compassion for poor whites who were penned up in the urban slums and whose labor kept the northern factories running.

Some political leaders like Ireland's Daniel O'Connell perceived a connection among oppressed people no matter where they lived. O'Connell, who was a champion of Irish independence, urged the Irish in America to side with the Blacks in the south and thereby advance the cause of human freedom. But his appeal was resented among the Irish in Boston and New York.

For all their misgivings, when the war actually began Catholics in the north were as quick to rally to their country's flag as anyone else. And—it must be added—so were Catholics in the south. There were Catholic privates, generals, and chaplains in both armies, according to the states where they lived. On both sides Catholic schools and orphanages were thrown open for use as emergency hospitals, frequently with the sisters serving as nurses.

President Abraham Lincoln, sensitive to the influence of Catholic opinion in Europe, asked Archbishop John J. Hughes of New York to cross the ocean and explain the Union position there. Hughes went readily. Not to be outdone, the Confederate government then asked Bishop Patrick Lynch of Charleston to make a similar trip explaining its position. Lynch also made the trip, but he received a less warm reception. The two bishops then exchanged a series of letters that summarized their opposing views. The letters, reprinted in newspapers in the north and south, didn't change anyone's mind, but they did reveal a high degree of mutual respect that was remarkable considering the bitterness of the times.

A slave cabin in the South. The official Catholic attitude toward slavery, while disapproving, was not as militant as Protestant abolitionists.

Father Thomas Mooney celebrates Mass for soldiers of the 69th Regiment during the Civil War.

The Immigrant and the War

The trouble was that the struggle between the Union and the Confederacy could not be maintained at a level where polite letters are exchanged between adversaries. There was fighting to be done and blood to be shed, a great deal of blood. The early expectations on both sides of a quick victory soon evaporated. The two peoples found themselves locked in a war that left tens of thousands of young men dead without any progress toward peace. It was a stalemate.

It was evident to everyone by this time that many more soldiers would be needed. Manpower was a resource that the north had more of than the south. The northern cities and factory towns were still crowded with men of service age, and if these didn't supply enough soldiers there were always newly-arrived immigrants. Recruiting offices were erected outside the landing depot at Castle Garden in New York where immigrants fresh off the boat were cajoled into joining the army for two years. More than one young soldier from Germany found himself dying for a nation he had lived in only a few weeks, whose flag he barely recognized, among people whose language he couldn't speak.

In the beginning military service was strictly voluntary. Thousands of immigrants signed up because they saw army service as a chance to prove their loyalty to the United States, their new homeland. Told that the war was being fought to preserve the Union, they willingly cooperated in the effort.

But then in 1862 the situation was subtly changed. President Lincoln, in an effort to enlist the moral support of Europe on the side of the Union, issued the Emancipation Proclamation which, in effect, changed the war from a struggle to preserve the Union into one to free the slaves. However noble the intention of the proclamation, it was bitterly resented in northern cities where people felt they were little better than slaves themselves.

Three months after the Emancipation Proclamation the battle of Fredericksburg was fought in Virginia. The Union army, spearheaded by several Irish regiments from New York, mounted a futile assault on a strong Confederate position. The losses were appalling. In two days 12,000 men were killed. Almost every New York Irish family knew of someone who had died.

Faced with such losses and the need to continue the war, the Federal government in 1863 passed the first draft law. According to the law, however, a person could legally avoid the draft if he could pay $300 for someone to fight in his place. Since it was difficult for the poor to come up with such a sum, the law had the effect of discriminating against the poorer classes.

In July of that year, through a mistake in assigning quotas, the great majority of draftees in New York were from Irish neighborhoods. That did it. The long pent-up resentments exploded. What began as a simple demonstration by Irish immigrants against the draft law turned into a riot. Mobs of angry citizens poured onto the streets. They attacked and burned the offices of Horace Greeley's *Tribune*, a newspaper sympathetic to the war. The Provost Marshall's office and other buildings were similarly attacked.

Sad to say, it was only a short step from burning buildings to looting and murder. Innocent Blacks were beaten on the street. At least one was lynched from a lamp post. And in another shameful episode an orphanage for Black children was burned to the ground.

For three days New York City was in a state of anarchy and mob rule, until soldiers were taken from combat positions to restore order in the streets. At the request of the government, Archbishop Hughes pulled himself from his sickbed and appealed to the crowd from his balcony. His priests followed his example, walking through the streets and pleading for order; so did the police, many of whom were also Irish. When it was all over sixty-six persons, including four Blacks, were left dead. It was a display of ugliness that would not soon be forgotten by other Americans.

War and Its Aftermath

The New York riots were never repeated, partly because in 1864 the war began to swing decisively in the Union's favor. The fighting now was carried deep into the south, from Tennessee down into Georgia, and from Fredericksburg into the heart of Virginia. The war became a brutal experience for families in the south, creating a condition of poverty that would last for generations.

Nor was the Church exempt from suffering and loss. Buildings were burned and diocesan treasures were depleted. Bishop William Elder of Natchez, Mississippi was expelled from the city for three weeks for refusing to allow occupation forces to dictate prayers in his churches. Bishop Lynch, who had gone to plead the Confederate cause in Europe, returned to find Charleston badly damaged by shellfire and his cathedral burned to the ground. Among his Catholics who needed help were 20,000 newly-freed Blacks. The bishop, as did many other clergymen, spent the rest of his life trying to rebuild.

In time, of course, the war ground to its inevitable finish. Weary troops like New York's 69th Regiment, composed largely of Irish soldiers, returned to their home cities with some measure of pomp and with the knowledge that at least no one could call them un-American any more.

On a national level the Catholic hierarchy reunited itself quickly and easily. Only eighteen months after the surrender document was signed at Appomattox, the bishops assembled in Baltimore for a plenary council to consider the problems of reconstruction. None of them, however, could foresee the real problems that lay ahead. If immigration had changed the Church drastically in the first half of the 19th century, it was due to change it even more radically in the second half. The big immigrations were just beginning.

8. The Golden Door

Thus far in this story of Catholics in America we have been referring often to immigration—how it triggered the Nativist movement, how it affected the Civil War, and how it changed the Catholic Church. Until now, however, we have not looked closely at immigration itself.

The very first pages of this book recalled how the

New World of America struck the first European explorers with awe. The beauty, the space, and the potential wealth of North America had an almost hypnotizing effect on the European mind. The American Revolution and the system of government that came out of it added to that attraction. To the poor European laborer, caught in the moribund social structures of his native land, the United States seemed to offer everything—political freedom and economic security. All he had to do was get there.

And from the very beginning the people came. In a sense, as John F. Kennedy observed, America is a land of immigrants. Everyone except the Indians can trace his origins back to some foreign place. Still, there has been a tendency for those who came *first* to feel themselves superior to those who came *later*. That attitude helps to explain much of the tension that was generated by immigration, both for the nation and for the Catholic Church.

At the time when the United States achieved its independence, Catholics made up less than one percent of the total population. The few Catholics who did live here were mostly English or Irish. They were economically equal to their Protestant neighbors and shared similar habits and attitudes. It was fairly easy for Bishop John Carroll to take steps which he expected would fully integrate his Church into American life.

But his plans would never be realized. First there were land acquisitions in the south and west which brought French-speaking and Spanish-speaking Catholics into the American population. And just as the Church was struggling to care for these, immigration from Europe began in earnest. The immigrants were quite unlike the aristocratic Carrolls. All too often they were poor, uneducated, lacking skills and social graces. Many of them, like the Irish, could speak English; but many others could not.

The movement started slowly at first, because sailing ships were small and transportation expensive. In 1820, 8,000 immigrants arrived in the United States. But by 1846 the number had increased to 90,000. Then, in 1847, famine struck Ireland. Hundreds of thousands of persons were faced with a grim choice of either leaving their country or staying to die. In the following year, 1848, political turmoil swept over Germany and central Europe, inducing many more thousands to emigrate.

Immigration by Decades	
Decade	Immigration by Decades
1820-1830	151,824
1831-1840	599,125
1841-1850	1,713,251
1851-1860	2,598,214
1861-1870	2,314,824
1871-1880	2,812,191
1881-1890	5,246,613
1891-1900	3,687,564
1901-1910	8,762,489
1911-1920	5,735,811
1921-1930	4,107,209
1931-1940	528,431
1941-1950	1,034,503
1951-1960	2,519,363
1961-1970	3,318,531
Total 1820-1970	45,129,943

In their best moments Americans pictured their country as an Ark offering safety and protection to the downtrodden peoples of the earth.

For those who had braved the ocean, the arrival in New York was a moment of joy mixed with the fear of possibly being sent home again.

We have already seen how immigration during this period gave rise to Nativism and other anti-immigrant feelings. On one hand America needed these new arrivals to expand its labor force. The entire 19th century was a period of tremendous economic growth in the United States—growth that would have been impossible without the cheap labor of the immigrants.

At the same time it was undeniably true that the immigrants were slowly changing the character of the American nation. This fact was bitterly resented by the long-time residents. They disliked the immigrants' religion, their politics, their customs, and their accents. Aware of this hostility, the immigrants tended to huddle together for mutual support in urban neighborhoods which evolved into ethnic ghettos. There they could practice their religion, speak their own language, and re-create a culture similar to that of the Old Country.

Varieties of Immigrants

Most European immigrants entered the United States at New York. Those who arrived prior to 1892 probably debarked at Castle Garden, a reception center at the tip of Manhattan Island. Those who came after that date were received at the Ellis Island depot in New York harbor. There they would undergo medical tests, have their papers checked, and usually purchase railroad or steamboat tickets for destinations elsewhere in the country.

For the vast majority of them the trip across the ocean had been uncomfortable, and in the early days often perilous. Most of them traveled in steerage, the cheapest way. The ships were dark and filthy. There was little privacy. The food was often abominable. One woman who arrived in 1828 wrote home to England, saying: "While we were passing over the water our sufferings were great . . . I will not grieve your hearts with all our sufferings, for my paper will not hold it. Little Mary was very ill with the fever that so many died with—seven children and one woman; to hear their cries and moans, it was very bad. I was so ill myself that I was forced to crawl out of my bed and lay on the floor while John made up the bed. If you know of any coming here, tell them never to come where the vessel is so full; for we were shut down in darkness for a fortnight, till so many died, then the hatch was opened. . . . We were about thirty-three days coming over, which was called a good passage."

Immigrants who came a few decades later, of course, had a much easier time crossing. But still there was anxiety when arriving in New York that the health inspector might detect a trace of tuberculosis or some other ailment and order the immigrant back to Europe. There were heartrending scenes when some family members were allowed in and others were turned away.

As we noted earlier, a large percentage of the first immigrants were Irish. Irish immigration peaked just before the Civil War. However, the Irish continued to flow in significant numbers for several decades thereafter.

Many Irish settled in cities along the eastern seaboard. German immigrants, on the other hand, tended to be wealthier than the Irish and better able to afford to purchase a tract of farmland in Pennsylvania or farther away in the midwest. They started businesses in cities like Milwaukee, St. Louis, or Cincinnati, which have a strong German flavor even today. They put down strong and durable roots, building churches, schools, and monasteries.

Because they settled in less populous areas and because most Germans did not initially speak English, they kept to themselves more than the Irish did, resisting assimilation. And because they were more withdrawn from the mainstream of American life the Germans suffered less prejudice at the hands of native-born Americans.

Many Irish and German immigrants, of course, didn't settle either in the east or the midwest. The discovery of gold in California occurred in 1848, corresponding to the first big wave of immigration. A fair percentage of the new Americans set off on a new trek across the plains, which for its hazards and hardships was just as difficult as the voyage across the ocean. Twenty years later the first transcontinental railroad was completed. After that the settlement of the west proceeded rapidly.

This period also marked the beginning of the second, and largest, surge of immigration into the United States. In the decade of the 1880s, five million persons came in the country—by far the largest number ever to arrive in a ten-year span. Then, in the first decade of the 20th century, eight million immigrants were admitted. When one considers that the total population of the U.S. at that time was only 75 million, one can imagine the effect eight million new arrivals had on the pattern of American life.

This latest migration had a different character than the one that preceded the Civil War. The earlier

Immigration by Country of Origin

Decade	Ireland[1]	Germany[2]	Russia[3]	Italy
1820-1830	54,338	7,729	89	439
1831-1840	207,381	152,454	277	2,253
1841-1850	780,719	434,626	511	1,870
1851-1860	914,119	951,667	457	9,231
1861-1870	435,778	787,468	2,512	11,725
1871-1880	436,871	718,182	39,284	55,759
1881-1890	655,482	1,452,970	213,282	307,309
1891-1900	388,416	505,152	505,290	651,893
1901-1910	339,065	341,498	1,597,306	2,045,877
1911-1920	146,181	143,925	921,957	1,109,524
1921-1930	220,591	412,202	89,423	455,315
1931-1940	13,167	114,058	7,401	68,028

[1] Includes Northern Ireland.
[2] Includes Austria, 1938-1940.
[3] Includes European Russia, Latvia, Estonia, Lithuania, and Finland.

immigrants were largely from northern and central Europe—Irish, English, Scandinavians, and Germans. The second wave of migrants tended to be from southern and eastern Europe. For the first time significant numbers of people came from Russia, Poland, and Italy. In the ten years following 1900, more than two million persons emigrated from Italy alone.

Naturally this tremendous influx of persons coming through the turnstiles at Ellis Island was bound to threaten the lifestyles of Americans already settled, including not a few Irish and Germans. The labor unions, which grew in power as the 20th century progressed, were also made uneasy by the continuing source of cheap labor. America in the wake of World War I was becoming more isolationist. There was a resurgence of Nativism in the air and a feeling that it was time to change the open admission policy for immigrants.

In 1924 Congress passed a law that limited immigration to 150,000 persons a year. The law had the effect of closing the door that had remained open for more than a century. It also had strong racist overtones, since it set quotas for allowable immigrants based on their natural origins. Northern Europeans were much more likely to gain admission than were southern or eastern Europeans or Orientals.

Thirty years after the Immigration Act was passed, Ellis Island was closed permanently. The great migrations to America had ended. Not until 1965 when the "national origins" quotas were removed by Congress did immigration begin to pick up again. Since then there has been a steady but not dramatic increase of immigration, especially from the Caribbean, Mexico, the Philippines, and Asia.

Probably never again will we see the huge numbers of arrivals that we saw at the turn of the century. We are beginning only now to appreciate the contributions those immigrants made to the American nation and to the American Catholic Church.

9. The Immigrant Church

The great masses of immigrants who poured into the United States in the hundred-year span that ended in 1924 radically altered the character of the American people. To an even greater extent it altered the character of the American Catholic Church. From being a tiny minority at the time of the American Revolution, Catholics had multiplied to the point where they made up the largest single religious body in the nation. From being largely English-speaking immigrants from the British Isles, Catholics now expressed themselves in many different languages and cultural styles. They could no longer hope to be assimilated quietly into the American nation. Instead, it would be the nation that would have to adjust.

Caring for the Immigrants

The most immediate task for the Catholic Church during this period was caring for the physical and spiritual needs of the immigrants. In the last thirty years of the 19th century the Catholic population in the United States shot up from 4.5 million persons to 12 million persons, and the Church's resources were stretched thin in an effort to provide for all their wants. This was in an age, remember, before the government welfare programs that we know today. The greatest burden of social care fell on private agencies like churches.

One service the Catholic Church provided was orphanages. In those days it was not unusual for families to become separated on the long journey from Europe, or for parents to die young from tuberculosis or despair in the urban ghettos. When this happened it was the Church, more often than not, that cared for the children.

Hospitals, too, were needed. And with no pensions or social security available to elderly persons, homes for the aged were another vital service. By 1900 the Church was operating more than 800 institutions of private charity, not counting schools.

Individual parishes organized St. Vincent de Paul Societies which collected clothing and sometimes provided hot meals for the poor.

As one might suspect, there were not nearly enough priests to provide the various ministries. Sisters and lay persons helped to take up the slack. One sister whose efforts stood above the others was born in Italy and at first was considered too frail for the rigorous life in the convent. In 1889 her bishop sent her to New York to see what she could do for the Italian immigrants there. Her name was Francesca Cabrini. The "frail" sister and the community of sisters she founded began a monumental service to the urban poor, establishing schools and building hospitals and orphanages on three continents. She crossed the ocean thirty times in the course of her work—despite the fact that she suffered from seasickness and despite recurrent attacks of malaria which finally caused her death. In 1946 Mother Cabrini was canonized a saint, the first American citizen to be so honored.

Efforts were also made at this time to help needy people outside the cities. The American Indians, who by no stretch of the imagination could be called immigrants, were in a desperate plight, having been driven from their tribal lands and harrassed by cavalry and settlers. The massacre at Wounded Knee, South Dakota, the last act of the tragic Indian Wars, took place in 1890. Four years before that Catholic parishes across the nation had begun annual collections to support the Indian missions. Yet the actual help that the immigrant Church could offer them was woefully small.

The same was true for American Blacks. In spite of the efforts of Mother Katherine Drexel and people like her, the Church was unable to do a great deal for Blacks newly freed after the Civil War. The care of immigrants was absorbing nearly all of the Church's energy. Some small steps were taken nonetheless. In 1875 James Healy, whose mother had been a slave, was appointed bishop of Portland, Maine. He was the first Black to serve in the American hierarchy. Some years later his brother, Jesuit Father Patrick Healy, became president of Georgetown University.

Work and Working Conditions

No matter how much the Church tried to alleviate the condition of immigrants, they were quickly swallowed up in the industrial boom that characterized late 19th century America. The Church brought them together on Sundays and cared for some of their wounds and ailments, but it could not protect the immigrants from the predatory aspects of capitalism which forced them into dingy slums and frightful working conditions.

There were no labor laws in those days to protect workingmen from on-the-job perils or to guarantee them an adequate wage in return for long hours of work. It was not unusual to find every member of an immigrant family working: Women would do sewing "piecework" at home or find jobs in dismal "sweat-shops"; children, too, worked in factories for what amounted to pennies a day. Even as late as the turn of the century it wasn't unusual to find boys eight and ten years old employed in cotton mills or doing heavy labor.

The cheap labor that was furnished by immigrants was a key ingredient to industrial growth in that period. Naturally this created instability in the labor force. Workingmen knew that if they got out of line they were easily replaced. It sometimes happened that blocks of newly-arrived immigrants were taken straight from their boats to factories whose regular workers had gone out on strike. And if, in spite of this threat, the workers still voted to strike, their rallies would be broken up by police and bullies hired by the employers.

Labor relations in the 19th century were not carried out in an atmosphere of negotiations and arbitration that we know today. When conflicts arose a century ago they frequently became violent. Consider the 1892 strike against the Homestead Steel Company which degenerated into full-scale warfare between the strikers and 300 armed guards brought in by the manufacturers. Even before that there was the case of the notorious Molly Maguires who for twenty years brought murder and terrorism to Pennsylvania's anthracite coal region. The fact that the Molly Maguires was a secret society composed largely of Irish Catholic laborers was duly noted in Nativist quarters where feelings against the Church still ran high. Eventually the organization was infiltrated by private detectives; its leaders were arrested and hanged.

There had been several attempts by this time to found organized trade unions that would protect the rights of workers. The trouble was, as soon as the union "went public" its members would be fired. And so most unions continued to keep their membership lists secret, as the Molly Maguires had. This element of secrecy, coupled with the immigrant origins of many union leaders, gave the whole movement a sinister air in the opinion of many Americans. Even many Church leaders were opposed to the idea of secrecy.

Secrecy, in fact, was one of the charges leveled against the Knights of Labor, a legitimate and nonviolent labor union directed by Terence V. Powderly. A onetime mayor of Scranton, Pennsylvania, Powderly led the union through a series of successful strikes until it reached the astonishing size of 700,000 members in 1886.

Trouble, however, was brewing for the Knights, and some of the trouble was coming from the Church. At the moment of the union's greatest strength, Cardinal Elezear Taschereau of Quebec convinced the Vatican to condemn the Knights in his diocese. Actually there were not many Knights *in* his diocese, but it seemed that Taschereau—who was from a wealthy, aristocratic family—was opposed to them on principle. There were several bishops in the United States who wanted to follow Taschereau's example, but they were brought up short by Cardinal James Gibbons of Baltimore.

This is the first time we have run into Gibbons, and it might be well to stop for a moment and consider the kind of a person he was. James Gibbons was born in Baltimore of Irish parents, and although he was educated in Ireland he returned to the United States to enter the seminary and be ordained a priest. He became a bishop at the early age of thirty-four, and as such he was the youngest bishop to attend the First Vatican Council. He was a friendly, mild-tempered man but a stout champion of individual freedom and democracy—both inside and outside the Church.

When opposition to the Knights of Labor began to grow, Gibbons agreed to meet privately with Powderly. He came away convinced that the union deserved the support of the Church, and he expressed his opinion in a letter to Pope Leo XIII. The American workingmen, he said, do not advocate "a democracy of license and violence, but true democracy which aims at the general prosperity through the means of sound principles and good social order."

The issue was left to Pope Leo. Several months went by. At last the pontiff issued a letter in which he declared that the Knights of Labor would not be condemned. Gibbons had won.

Four years later the Pope issued his famous encyclical letter *Rerum Novarum*, the first of the modern social encyclicals, which came out squarely for the rights of workingmen, including the right to a decent

Above, the Church provided charitable service in an age when there were no government welfare programs. This is a home for "fallen women" in New York. Archbishop Gibbons of Baltimore, right, rose to become America's first cardinal and a revered figure in public life.

wage and the right to organize unions.

The dispute over the Knights of Labor was an important moment in the history of the American Catholic Church. Cardinal Gibbons and Pope Leo XIII had made it clear that henceforth the Church would be on the side of the workingman. This was heartening news for the immigrants who made up a large portion of the nation's work force.

In Europe the Catholic Church was well on its way to losing the loyalty of the working classes. But the quick action of Gibbons had assured that this would not happen in North America. Working people would remain in the Church. In time they would become a powerful influence in the labor movement, in business, and in government.

In ways like this the Catholic Church gave support to its immigrant members and helped to make them full, participating members of the American society.

IV
Americanization
Versus Romanization

10. The Americanizers

The flood of immigration poured unabated into the United States during the whole last half of the 19th century. It overflowed the big cities of the eastern seaboard, spilled into the rich farmlands of the midwest and the Great Plains and continued to roll all the way to the Pacific coast. Every place the immigrants settled was transformed by their presence.

And just as the immigrants changed the character of the towns and cities they lived in, so they changed the Catholic Church. Where once the Church was fairly uniform in its composition, it was now more like a quilt of differing (and sometimes clashing) traditions. One was not merely a Catholic any longer; one was an Irish Catholic, or a Polish Catholic, or a Hungarian Catholic. Where once Catholics had been *religiously* different from mainstream, Protestant Americans, they were now religiously *and ethnically* different.

The only label that was hard to apply to them was "American Catholic." Because, really, what is an American Catholic? To what extent does being an

American add anything to one's Catholic faith? To what extent does America have a distinct culture that can nurture the faith the way, for instance, the Polish culture has done, or the Italian culture?

Questions of this sort are still being asked by Catholics today. But the way they were asked and answered in the last years of the 19th century brought on an ideological struggle that affected the American Church right up to Vatican II.

The Movement of Americanization

In the years following the Civil War, Catholic intellectuals began to give a great deal of thought to the relationship between the Church and the American culture. On one side there were those who felt uneasy with American-style "pluralism" which gives all religions equal recognition. Catholics in this camp felt that the Church should insist on its distinctiveness and keep itself separate from the general society.

On the other side there were those who felt just as strongly that the Church should be fully immersed in the American way of life, welcoming the innovations it finds and learning from them. In this way, they argued, the Church would have the greatest possible impact on secular society.

This conflict in views arose when it did because the late 19th century was a period of intense national pride. The United States was beginning to realize its military and economic strength. People were talking about America's "manifest destiny" to be a world leader, assuming as they did that American intentions were always honest and just. They sincerely believed that American democracy was the highest possible form of civil government. Wasn't it natural, then, that other societies—even the Church—should learn from America's example? To a growing number of Catholics the answer to that question was "yes."

Typical of these so-called "Americanizers" was a young New York priest named Edward McGlynn. McGlynn was a vigorous man, a dynamic speaker, handsome, and with a charm that attracted people to his leadership. He was also a prominent social reformer. Following the Civil War he had ministered to Irish squatters living in shanties in Central Park. The experience had left him with a deep concern for the poor and the working classes.

Around McGlynn was organized an informal group of ten or so priests known as the "Academia." Progressive both in politics and Church affairs, these priests wanted to reconsider traditional Catholic practices such as clerical celibacy, clerical dress, the Latin Mass, and the continuance of the Papal States. They took many of their ideas from Europe's liberal Catholics who were trying to modify the reactionary stance their Church had adopted ever since the French Revolution.

But the American progressives, like the priests in the Academia, went one step further than their European cousins. They began to argue that American society offered the possibility of a unique relationship with the Church. By 1867 McGlynn was propounding what the Academians called their "American idea." The idea was simple: the United States, if it wanted to be true to its own heritage, had to become Catholic.

No one did more to put this "American idea" into practice than an extraordinary young convert named Isaac Hecker. Hecker was an intellectual with a mystical bent who had first sought enlightenment from the Transcendentalists in Massachusetts. He was a friend of Ralph Waldo Emerson and Henry David Thoreau, and had even spent some time living at Brook Farm, a utopian commune outside Boston that was favored by the Transcendentalists. Then in 1844 Hecker became a Catholic.

A few years later, after studying for the priesthood in Europe and being ordained a priest in the Redemptorist Congregation, Hecker returned to the United States. Some years later he left the Redemptorists to found the Paulist Fathers, the first community of priests established by an American. With their help he set out to do what the Academia talked about—to convert America to Catholicism. He wrote books, he founded a magazine called *Catholic World,* and he gave innumerable lectures to Catholic and Protestant audiences. Over and over he repeated his theme: Catholic theology does not regard human beings as fallen or inherently sinful (as did some Protestant reformers), and therefore Catholicism has much in common with American democracy.

Inevitably Hecker failed to turn all Americans into Catholics. Yet he was a tremendously influential figure, both inside and outside the Church. He was the first Catholic apologist to approach Americans with complete respect for their traditions. Within the Catholic community he promoted the American notion of personal initiative; the priests of his community were encouraged to follow their own interests and inspirations. In addition they were bound to-

Isaac T. Hecker, left, friend of Emerson and Thoreau, and founder of the Paulists. Orestes Brownson, right, a man sometimes hard to get along with, but an important political and religious thinker in his day.

The First faculty of the Catholic University of America. Bishop John J. Keane stands in the center, rear.

gether by promises, not the traditional vows.

An American Catholic Renaissance

The emergence of people like Hecker and McGlynn who were unafraid to stand up and be identified as Catholics signalled a new era of self-confidence within the Catholic community. People were beginning to surmount their immigrant beginnings and to take larger and more aggressive roles in American life. They made contributions in the intellectual sphere, in politics, journalism, and art.

One such figure was Orestes Brownson who, like Hecker, was a disciple of the Transcendentalists and a convert to Catholicism. Through the pages of *Brownson's Quarterly Review* he exerted a considerable influence on Boston's intellectual life, commenting on such fields as art, politics, philosophy, and religion. Brownson had a first-rate mind, marred only by his tendency to lapse into heated controversy. Nevertheless, he gave thirty years of his life to the task of explaining Catholicism to American Protestants.

A fellow Bostonian, at this time, was John Boyle O'Reilly who used the pages of the *Boston Pilot* to campaign for Blacks and laborers. O'Reilly also gained a reputation as a poet. In New York, two journalists named James McMaster and Maurice Egan helped to make *The Freeman's Journal* the closest thing Catholics had to a national newspaper in the late 19th century. In the same city John Gilmary Shea edited the *Catholic News* while working simultaneously on his monumental history of the American Catholic Church.

In the arts, John LaFarge gained a reputation as a painter. So did George Healey. And Patrick Healy was well known as an architect.

During the Civil War students were already on campuses at Boston College, Dayton, and Notre Dame. The decades after the war saw an even greater boom in Catholic higher education. The Jesuits founded a succession of urban colleges from one coast to another that brought learning to the sons of immigrants in the big cities.

Catholic Colleges Founded 1870-1899

Date	College	Place
1870	Canisius College	Buffalo, N.Y.
	Loyola University	Chicago, Ill.
	St. John's University	Brooklyn, N.Y.
1871	Ursuline College	Cleveland, Ohio
	Chestnut Hill College	Philadelphia, Pa.
1872	Maryville College	St. Louis, Mo.
	St. Peter's College	Jersey City, N.J.
1873	Notre Dame College of Md.	Baltimore, Md.
1876	St. Edward's University	Austin, Tex.
1877	Detroit University	Detroit, Mich.
1878	Belmont Abbey College	Belmont, N.C.
	Creighton University	Omaha, Neb.
	Duquesne University	Pittsburgh, Pa.
1881	Incarnate Word College	San Antonio, Tex.
	Marquette University	Milwaukee, Wis.
1882	St. Ambrose College	Davenport, Ia.
1883	Seton Hall College	Greensburg, Pa.
1884	St. Francis College	Brooklyn, N.Y.
1885	College of St. Thomas	St. Paul, Minn.
	University of San Francisco	San Francisco, Cal.
1886	John Carroll University	Cleveland, Ohio

Catholic Colleges Founded 1870-1899

Date	College	Place
1887	Gonzaga University	Spokane, Wash.
1888	Regis College	Denver, Colo.
	University of Scranton	Scranton, Pa.
1889	Catholic University of America	Washington, D.C.
	St. Anselm's College	Manchester, N.H.
	St. Joseph's College	Rensselaer, Ind.
	St. Leo College	St. Leo, Fla.
1890	St. Procopius College	Lisle, Ill.
	College of St. Rafael	St. Rafael, Cal.
1891	Seattle University	Seattle, Wash.
1892	St. Bernard College	St. Bernard, Ala.
1895	St. Martin's College	Olympia, Wash.
1896	Notre Dame College	St. Louis, Mo.
1897	Trinity College	Washington, D.C.
1898	St. Norbert College	West St. Pere, Wis.
	De Paul University	Chicago, Ill.
1899	College of St. Elizabeth	Convent Station, N.J.

There was a movement afoot, too, to raise the educational standards of Catholic seminaries. The typical American priest was no longer a circuit-riding missionary. More likely he was stationed in a large city where—although he ministered primarily to the poorer classes—he was expected to show some sophistication. The clergy needed to be men of learning.

Back in 1859 the bishops had founded the North American College, a residence in Rome where American seminarians lived while going to school. Two decades later the college had been granted pontifical status and was gaining a reputation under its progressive young rector, Msgr. Denis O'Connell. But the North American College was not enough. What was needed was a first-rate center for learning in the United States. This led to the foundation in 1889 of the Catholic University of America in Washington, D.C.

The creation of Catholic University was prompted in large part by the foresight and persistence of John Lancaster Spaulding, bishop of Peoria, Illinois. Being an intellectual, Spaulding was frankly distressed at the isolation of Catholic ideas in America. He wanted the university to be a kind of bridge between American democracy and Catholic culture. In that regard he faithfully reflected the "Americanizing" ideas operating in the Church at the time. His vision was fully shared by Bishop John J. Keane, the university's first rector, who was a champion of religious pluralism. Keane led a Catholic delegation to the "Parliament of Religions" at the Columbia Exposition in Chicago in 1892. He also accepted an invitation to preach at Harvard.

The truth is, by the last decade of the 19th century the love affair some Catholic intellectuals had for the American way of life was becoming positively euphoric. Foremost among them was Archbishop John Ireland of St. Paul, a feisty and influential member of the hierarchy, who rhapsodized to the effect that the United States separation of Church and State was the ideal arrangement for the modern world. The Church and State, he said, were like body and soul. There should be no distinction between the love bestowed upon one or the other.

Ireland's sentiments were echoed—and, if possible, expanded on—by Cardinal James Gibbons who declared that the United States Constitution was "the most noble document ever written by the hand of man." Gibbons was lauded in turn by his great and good friend President Theodore Roosevelt who described the cardinal as "the most venerated, respected, and useful citizen in our country."

By the turn of the century it appeared that Gibbons and the Americanizing faction in the Church were succeeding in their efforts to create an era of good feeling between Catholicism and the secular state. If each individual citizen would not be baptized as Isaac Hecker wished, then it seemed that the Church was willing to baptize the American way of life.

However, there were dangers involved in that process, and as time went on those dangers began to create problems for the Church.

11. Conservative Reaction

Inevitably the movement to "Americanize" the Church spawned a reaction. There were people inside the Church who believed that any attempt to ally the Church with liberal democracy threatened its divine character. This reaction began to assert itself on both sides of the Atlantic, but in order to understand it best we should look at its European roots.

Pius IX was elected to the papacy in June of 1846 as a moderate progressive, seemingly in tune with the winds of change then blowing through Europe. Two years later the continent was swept by revolution. Kings and princes were overthrown. Rag-tag armies marched against the tottering monarchies that traced their ancestry to medieval times. One of the targets of this new liberation movement was the

Papal States in central Italy. The pope was forced to flee from Rome, and the once-progressive Pius IX became overnight a staunch conservative.

In 1864 the pope issued a "Syllabus of Errors" that condemned many modern ideas—including the notion that the papacy ought to align itself with progress. And five years after that he called an ecumenical council. Pius knew he would soon lose the last of the Papal States. He was fearful that the nationalistic spirit of the day might induce national blocs of bishops to overrule a pope who was shorn of temporal power. So Pius induced the bishops of that First Vatican Council to declare that a pope, when he formally defines a matter of faith or morals, is infallible and cannot be overruled.

Some American bishops at the council felt the definition was ill-timed, believing that it would only inspire anti-Catholic sentiment in the United States. But in the end only one American—Bishop Edward Fitzgerald of Little Rock—voted against the dogma. On one hand the council was recognized as a diplomatic triumph for the pope. However, it did have the effect of placing the Church more securely in the camp of the conservatives, and in time it became increasingly difficult for Catholics to dialogue with liberal thinkers.

The Conservative Bloc in America

In the decade after the First Vatican Council a significant group of conservative prelates began to form in the United States. Bishops of the previous generation—men like John Hughes—had finally overcome the threat of lay trusteeism in Catholic parishes. Now their successors were determined to maintain a strong, centralized control of Church affairs. The new declaration of infallibility strengthened their hands inasmuch as it tended to make the faithful more docile and obedient to Church authority.

One of the leaders of the conservative bloc was Bishop Bernard McQuaid of Rochester. McQuaid was a vigorous champion of Catholic education, having founded Seton Hall College in New Jersey and built some forty parochial schools in his upstate New York diocese.

Even more influential than McQuaid was Archbishop Michael Corrigan of New York City. Corrigan's father had been an Irish immigrant who became wealthy in the grocery and liquor business. Young Michael studied for the priesthood at the new North American College in Rome during the period of Vatican retrenchment. Once ordained, he taught at Seton Hall under McQuaid, was consecrated bishop of Newark, and in 1885 became Archbishop of New York.

As a bishop, Corrigan had little contact with or sympathy for working-class Catholics. He had had little pastoral experience. He was opposed to the social activism of priests like Edward McGlynn. Unlike McGlynn and Isaac Hecker, he felt he had to choose between American values and the Catholic faith; he could not make them fit together. He distrusted popular democracy, once writing: "There is more reason to dread anarchy than tyranny in the United States."

As conservative bishops became more upset at the growing liberalism of the Church, they looked for a way to reinforce their governing structures. They found it at Baltimore in 1884 during the Third Plenary Council of American Bishops. At Baltimore the hierarchy drew up a blueprint for a Catholic subculture that in a few decades would be institutionalized into a Catholic ghetto, which has sometimes been called the Baltimore Catechism Church. The name is derived from the new catechism the bishops approved at the meeting. They also ordered parochial schools built in all American parishes.

It would be wrong to think that only conservatives backed these measures. Under Cardinal Gibbons' calm guidance, the decrees represented a consensus of what all the bishops believed necessary for their rapidly-growing Church. Indeed, the Plenary Council marked a high-water mark of unity among the bishops. Almost immediately afterward the hierarchy was rent by disagreements. The first of these was the German issue.

By the 1880s there were more German Catholics than Irish Catholics entering the United States. In some cities like Milwaukee, St. Louis, and Cincinnati German-Americans made up the majority of the population. Yet the American hierarchy was still predominantly Irish. There had been few German bishops—St. John Neumann of Philadelphia being an exception.

These German Catholics had a fierce pride in their religious heritage. Many had been driven from their homeland because of persecutions. They were deeply loyal to the Church. Because so many of them had settled in the cities and farmlands of the middle west—far from the assimilating influences of the eastern cities—they tended to retain their language and traditional customs. They were a cultured people. They came together in the Benedictine abbeys of Minnesota and Indiana where the centuries-old love of liturgy and learning was preserved. The Germans had a slogan that said "language saves the faith." They believed that by retaining the German language in churches, schools, and newspapers they were protecting their Catholic faith from being watered-down and secularized.

Those who wanted to Americanize the Catholic Church looked at the German experience with skepticism. They were afraid that the nationalistic spirit of the Germans would only heighten Protestant suspicions that Catholics were less than fully American. Indeed, there was something about the Germans that seemed to irritate the Irish—and vice versa. Small issues began to cause bickering between them. For instance some Irish prelates, like Archbishop Ireland of St. Paul, favored total abstinence from liquor; the Germans, who were fairly moderate drinkers and who controlled the beer industry, resented Ireland's support of prohibition.

Schools, National Parishes, Politics

Several other issues pitted the Germans against the Irish and the liberals against the conservatives in the early 1890s. The most important of these involved parochial schools.

In a speech to the National Educational Association in St. Paul, Archbishop Ireland declared that the state had the primary responsibility to educate children, and what is more he suggested that parochial schools be leased to the state on a shared-time basis. Immediately he came under fire from two quarters. Many Protestants said Ireland's suggestion was part of a Catholic plot to take over the public schools. Some Catholics, especially German Catholics, charged that Ireland was trying to destroy the parochial school system. One German layman issued a warning to those who sought to "give our parish schools over to unbelievers for a price."

While the school issue was simmering, German Catholics were continuing their own campaign to have more Germans appointed to the hierarchy and to have some measure of autonomy for German-speaking parishes. The issue of autonomy for national parishes was a sensitive one. Having recently won the battle against lay trusteeism, the Irish-dominated hierarchy was not about to sanction a new collection of independent parishes in their dioceses.

Leading the fight for national parishes was a German lay organization called the St. Raphael Society which was originally created to help German immigrants in the United States. Under the vigorous leadership of a German layman, Peter Paul Cahensely, the society did an immense amount of good for the poorer classes of Germans, and it served as a lobby for German Catholics generally. In 1890 the society petitioned Rome once more for additional German bishops and parishes. Because the petition originated at a St. Raphael's meeting in Switzerland it infuriated Archbishop Ireland. He accused Cahensely unjustly of conspiring with the German government to "foreignize" the American Church. For months afterward Irish Catholics were warning darkly about the dangers of "Cahenselyism," and even Cardinal

Gibbons was distressed enough to ask Rome to ignore the petition.

As if this were not enough to occupy the attention of liberals and conservatives, one final fight erupted that riveted the attention not only of Catholics but of all Americans. It happened in New York City and pitted Archbishop Corrigan against that unruly social activist, Father James McGlynn.

McGlynn in 1886 was supporting the political aspirations of Henry George in an election for mayor of New York City. George was an economist with pronounced socialist leanings. Believing that excessive rents were an unfair burden on the poor, he wanted the state to control the ownership of land—and perhaps in time to abolish privately-owned real estate. Such notions frightened Archbishop Corrigan, who believed they were contrary to Church teaching. He could do nothing about Henry George, a non-Catholic, but he could, and did, order Father McGlynn to cease his support of George. McGlynn refused and was suspended. Then when the priest declined to go to Rome to defend himself he was excommunicated by the pope.

It was a sad situation. McGlynn was a popular figure among most rank-and-file Catholics. Cardinal Gibbons, Archbishop Ireland, and Bishop Keane at Catholic University tried to intervene on his behalf. Their efforts only angered Corrigan. Letters flew back and forth across the Atlantic. Charges and recriminations flooded the newspapers. Six years after the council of Baltimore, that was remarkable for its wonderful unity, the American Church was in a state of disarray.

Pope Leo XIII clearly had to do something about

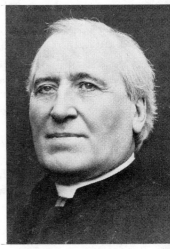

Archbishop Michael Corrigan, left, of New York. He thought the Americanizers were going too far. Archbishop John Ireland of St. Paul, right. He wanted the state to take over parochial schools.

The war with Spain in 1898 made leaders in Europe, including the Vatican, uneasy about the power of the U.S. This is the naval battle of Santiago.

the situation. In 1892 he sent Archbishop Francesco Satolli to the United States as his personal representative to gather information about the various disputes and bring some degree of order out of the chaos. The Italian prelate arrived on a cloud of goodwill and proceeded to talk to all sides. Then he issued his report.

The conservatives were astounded. "In the name of the Pope" Satolli settled the school controversy along lines that basically favored Archbishop Ireland's plan. One month later he declared that Father McGlynn's political ideas did not deny Church teaching. The New York priest was reinstated. At Satolli's suggestion, Rome also turned down the German request for more national parishes. On nearly every issue it appeared that the liberals had triumphed. They were ecstatic. There was a feeling in the air that the Catholic Americanizers were on the verge of triumph. So great was their confidence that Archbishop Ireland and Msgr. Denis O'Connell left on a trip to carry the "American gospel" to France.

It seemed the Americanizers had every reason to be optimistic. Appearances, however, were deceiving. The big battles were still to be fought.

12. Conservative Triumph

Midway through the 1890s it appeared that the wounds in the American Church were well on their way to being healed. Archbishop Satolli, the pope's representative in America, was a popular figure. So successful was his mission that in 1893 a permanent Apostolic Delegation was established in Washington to give the Vatican a "listening post" in the United States. Steps were already being taken to end America's designation as a "mission territory" and to give it equal status with other national Churches.

But not everything was as calm as it seemed, nor was Satolli as progressive as he first appeared. Increasingly, as a time went on, the new Apostolic Delegate tended to support the positions of Bishop McQuaid and Archbishop Corrigan.

The first break came with a Vatican document which strongly reinforced the practice of separate parochial schools and implicitly criticized the ideas of Archbishop Ireland who had wanted to lease the schools to the state.

Following on the heels of this, another letter from the pope warned Americans against too many contacts with Protestants. It appeared to be aimed at Bishop Keane's participation in the Parliament of Religions at Chicago a short time earlier, but indirectly it seemed to attack the very notion of American religious pluralism.

Then Bishop Keane himself was asked to resign as rector of the Catholic University. The pope, it seems, had bowed to the wishes of conservatives who were fearful of Keane's progressive ideas. Only the year before Msgr. Denis O'Connell had been forced out as rector of the North American College in Rome. That meant the liberals had lost the two positions most influential in the education of new priests.

By this time Archbishop Satolli, now a cardinal, was back in Rome. Looking around for a party to blame, the liberals decided that the German Catholics were behind these moves of the Vatican. There was an exchange of nasty charges in the secular press, which was only too happy to oblige the warring prelates. Rumors abounded. One such rumor held that Bishop McQuaid was about to be removed from his see in Rochester because of his feud with Archbishop Ireland. The story proved to be false.

The Americanism "Heresy"

While this was going on in America, a problem of a different sort had appeared in France. In 1897 a French edition of the life of Isaac Hecker was published in Paris. The book contained a new introduction, written by a Frenchman, that made the American priest seem far more radical than he really was. Before long French liberals became all excited about "Americanism"—by which they meant an arrangement that freed the Church from old structures and opened it up to modern progress. In some circles Hecker was being hailed as a saint. To conservatives he seemed a heretic.

In the midst of these philosophical struggles, another kind of warfare broke out in the Caribbean. It was a shooting war this time, pitting the United States against Catholic Spain. Almost inevitably European conservatives found themselves favoring Spain. In the United States, however, liberal and conservative Catholics were wholeheartedly on the American side; indeed, for some of them, it seemed like a struggle between the old and the new civilizations. As Msgr. O'Connell wrote: "It is a question of all that is old and vile and mean and rotten and cruel and false in Europe, against all that is free and noble and open and true and humane in America." The

Catholics cheered when Cuba fell to American soldiers; they cheered when the Philippines were wrenched from Spanish hands at Manila Bay.

All these developments proved too much for Pope Leo. In January of 1899 he sent a public letter to Cardinal Gibbons condemning those ideas being spread around Europe under the heading of "Americanism." The letter was a blow to the liberals. They took comfort only in the fact that Hecker was not condemned and that the pope found many aspects of the American Church worthy of praise. Also, no one was being charged with heresy—a fact that Gibbons was quick to point out. But the letter was clearly a warning against any attempt to make the American values of self-initiative, democracy, and freedom a part of Church life. In effect, the pope was telling American liberals that they had misunderstood his gestures toward democracy. They had no commission to "Americanize" the Church.

While the conservatives were pleased by these developments, it would not be true to say that the liberal movement was stopped in its tracks. In some respects it was just reaching fruition. There was great intellectual ferment at Catholic University and at diocesan seminaries. Dunwoodie Seminary in New York began in 1905 to publish *The New York Review*, a thoroughly up-to-date journal of religion. The seminary boasted an outstanding faculty assembled by Archbishop John Farley, Corrigan's successor.

But in the long run, no collection of scholars in New York or Washington would be able to shield the Church from its collision with the modern world. Events were already moving too fast, and when the final contest came the petty arguments between liberals and conservatives in America would count for little.

The showdown occurred in Europe. Toward the end of the 19th century Christian thinkers, both Protestant and Catholic, began to apply some new methods to old theological problems. These included the use of strict historical criteria in Bible studies, and applying the notion of "evolution" to Church dogma. These "Modernists," as they were called, seemed to imply that religious truth was not as clear and definite as it was once thought to be. In the forefront of the movement were Catholics Maurice Blondel and Alfred Loisy in France and George Tyrrell in England.

Pope Leo XIII, an old man then, had hesitated to take action against the movement. But in 1903 he was succeeded by Pope Pius X, a saintly but determined leader who was theologically more conservative than Leo. He issued a series of letters culminating with the encyclical *Pascendi* in 1907 which condemned the movement and all its manifestations. Priests all over the world were compelled to take an oath against Modernism, and some men—including Loisy and Tyrell—were excommunicated.

For the American Church—and indeed for the Church as a whole—the condemnation had a chilling effect. Only a half dozen American priests actually held the beliefs that were condemned, but progressives everywhere were put on the defensive. Seminary faculties were purged. *The New York Review* was discontinued. Liberals were warned to keep silent or devote themselves to non-theological pursuits. Father John Zahm, a physicist at Notre Dame, was disciplined for accepting the theory of evolution and thereafter confined himself to writing travel books.

So what had promised to be an intellectual flowering among American Catholics in the 20th century became instead a withering. Theologians stopped arguing with each other, battles between bishops quieted down, and all sides looked for activities that were safe and non-controversial.

The Reform of Canon Law

One other event helped to stop the Americanizing process in the Catholic Church, and that was the reform of the Church's canon law in 1918. Before we look at the effect it had, it might be wise to consider the issues that were at stake.

We tend to think that all law is pretty much the same. It specifies a few things that we must not do, but for the most part leaves us free to do as we please. Americans, who are raised in this tradition, tend to obey their laws to the letter, without exceptions, knowing that they still have large areas of freedom. Roman law, however, operates under a slightly different principle than the common law system of America. Roman law attempts to set down general guidelines for all aspects of human behavior. Although it deals with a wider range of activities, Roman law is more loose and makes room for a variety of exceptions and dispensations.

Some Americans had been urging the Vatican to restructure Church law in the British and American common law pattern. But the Romans would have none of it; they used their own system. When the new canon law was put into practice, American Catholics felt bound to obey it to the letter—since that is the way they obeyed their own law. They bowed to every rule and regulation, and soon became famous in the Church for their excessive legalism. They became more Romanized than the Romans.

The cumulative effect of all these developments— the reform of canon law, the condemnation of Americanism and then of Modernism—was to swing the power in the American Church to the side of the conservatives. Looking back, the outcome was probably a mixed blessing. If the Americanizers had succeeded in adapting the Church completely to secular American society, the Church might well have lost its distinctiveness, if not its soul. The optimistic, turn-of-the-century patriotism which viewed the United States as the answer to all the world's problems and which so inspired the Americanists seems naive to us today.

Yet on the other hand the victory of the conservatives was enormously costly. Although the United States was graduating from the status of a mission land, it was actually becoming more and more dependent on Rome. The Apostolic Delegate, living in Washington, carefully monitored the appointment of new American bishops. The national hierarchy virtually ceased to exist as a policy-forming body. Conformism was the rule in American parishes and schools. Creative ideas were stifled in colleges and seminaries.

The institutional growth of the Church during the period served to maintain the status quo. Parochial schools assumed a great importance, but they re-

Pope Pius X was a saintly man, but one who believed in a firm exercise of papal authority.

quired large parishes to support them—parishes where many people barely knew their priests. And as the Church bureaucracy grew to accommodate the proliferating institutions, bishops and pastors were selected more and more on the basis of their administrative and financial talents.

In time, the petty differences that gave rise to the conflicts of the late 19th century disappeared. The distinctions between Germans and Irish gradually dissolved. The personalities who led the various factions died and were forgotten. The older dilemma of what it meant to be an American Catholic was resolved for the time being by a process of compartmentalization. Henceforth a Catholic was free to participate fully in American society, but his Catholic identity had little to do with his American identity. It seemed that his religious experience no longer illuminated his larger social experience.

Isaac Hecker's dream that America and Catholicism might blend together and strengthen each other was fading. By 1920 it appeared unlikely that the dream would be revived.

V
The Modern Era

13. State of Siege

As the United States moved well into the 20th century, its Catholic citizens took a new breath and turned away from the internal bickering that had disrupted its life in the previous two or three decades. Their attention was given less to theoretical issues and more to practical ones. The struggles over Americanism and modern criticism were not settled but postponed. The time was not right for solutions.

In the meantime, their growing Church needed attention. In the thirty-five years between 1880 and 1915 the number of Catholics in the United States had jumped from six million to fifteen million. They had 20,000 priests to look after their spiritual welfare, and many times that number of Religious. The new parishes and parochial schools that seemed to be springing up everywhere needed a veritable army of caretakers.

In fact, the army image was a popular one among Catholics. Increasingly they saw themselves as a "Church militant"—as a mighty, intractable army of believers. They were not an inspired, conquering army, ready to convert America, as Isaac Hecker had wished. Rather they were a proud, aloof army, guarding the fortress of their Church, protecting their children and their faith from the evils of assimilation. They were the army of a city under siege.

The Church and Popular Culture

This unconscious decision of Catholics to hold themselves apart from the mainstream of American life could be seen in the array of separate institutions they created for themselves. Not only were there Catholic schools and churches, there were Catholic boy scouts and girl scouts, Catholic lawyers' guilds and doctors' guilds, Catholic summer camps, Catholic societies to promote agriculture, and poetry, and economics, and journalism—all of which copied identical societies in the secular world.

Even though immigration dropped off sharply in the 1920s, the parish continued to be the focal point of social life for Catholics. The men were likely to attend the Holy Name Society or the Knights of Columbus (which had been founded in New Haven, Connecticut, back in 1882), while the women joined the Altar or Rosary Society. For entertainment they attended parish bazaars and dances. They never got married without first conferring with their priests, and only the bravest of them contracted a "mixed marriage" with a non-Catholic.

The fact that they stayed to themselves did not mean Catholics lacked devotion to their country. If anything, they tended to be even more patriotic than the average American, thereby attempting to prove that their loyalty to Rome did not affect their allegiance to the United States. The Broadway actor and song-writer George M. Cohan typified the super-patriotism of Irish-Americans with songs like "Grand Old Flag," and "I'm a Yankee Doodle Dandy." With the outbreak of World War I young Catholic men who were only one or two generations removed from their European roots rushed to enlist. Cohan cranked out "Over There."

The war was a healing experience for American Catholics. Not only did it give them another opportunity to prove their patriotism, but within the Church it served to unite Germans and Irish, liberals and conservatives. Father Francis Duffy, who had been an editor of the daringly progressive *New York Review*, now became Father Francis Duffy, chaplain of the "Fighting 69th Regiment." His statue, in a military uniform, can be seen today in New York's Times Square.

After the war, however, America returned to its old Nativist ways—a development that boded ill for Catholics. The nation rejected President Woodrow Wilson's dream for a League of Nations, preferring to remain insular, suspicious of foreign elements. The Russian revolution in 1917 had profoundly frightened many citizens. They strove relentlessly to rid the nation of alien influences—which frequently led to the persecution of foreign-looking immigrants. Attorney General Mitchell Palmer directed a series of highly-publicized "raids" against supposed anarchists. And in Massachusetts two men named Nicola Sacco and Bartolomeo Vanzetti, immigrant laborers who admitted to being anarchists, were convicted and executed for a murder they may have committed, but probably did not.

The national consciousness was being armed against aliens, legally and illegally. The Immigration Act of 1924 virtually shut off the flow of new

This anti-Smith cartoon purports to show a cabinet meeting "if Al were President." Smith, right, brings in a jug of whiskey for the assembled prelates.

Knute Rockne, left, typified the self-image of Catholics in the 1920s: honest, passionate, strong. Alfred E. Smith, right, had a distinguished record as governor of New York before he ran for President in 1928.

arrivals at Ellis Island. In the south and midwest the Ku Klux Klan rode once more, preaching hatred against Blacks, Jews, and Catholics. By 1924 the Klan claimed a membership of five million Americans.

These new Nativists of the 1920s also thought the country would be a cleaner, better place if only they could do away with intoxicating drinks. The Eighteenth Amendment, establishing prohibition, went into effect in 1920. Millions of immigrant Catholics whose families had grown up with wine or beer in the old country resented what they felt to be a Puritan mentality behind the legislation. With some, it went beyond resentment. Organized gangsters flourished. The presence among them of names like "Bugs" Moran and Al Capone was not a good advertisement for ethnic Americans.

Catholics on the whole condemned the gangsterism and law-breaking just as vehemently as Protestants did. Catholic parents warned their children about the evils of roadsters and bathtub gin. They looked with a stern and disapproving eye at the desperate gaiety of the Roaring Twenties and wanted none of it. The kind of scenes being portrayed, for instance, on the neighborhood movie screens led to the founding of the Legion of Decency. Each year Catholics were asked to stand up in church and pledge themselves not to see any movie the Legion frowned upon.

For most citizens the postwar period was a time of great creative ferment, especially in the areas of music and literature. The Catholic Church, however, contributed little to secular art or ideas. It did not allow jazz into its sanctuary where the priest still faced the altar. Those Catholics who succeeded in the arts had, for the most part, left the Church. Men like Eugene O'Neill, Theodore Dreiser, and F. Scott an intellectual was still thirty years

New Social Consciousness

...earlier, the condemnation of Modern-
...t decade of the 20th century had a
...n the intellectual life of the Church.
...ch among theologians was frowned
...ally dangerous. As a result, creative
...hurch began to seek other outlets for
...and one of the most obvious outlets
...n.

...was not an entirely new discovery for
...olics. We have already seen how Car-
...nd others had championed the rights
... in the previous century. The Church
...a leader in the realm of private charity,
...s of hospitals, orphanages, and other
...ng from coast to coast. Father Edward
...Boys Town near Omaha, Nebraska,
...at priest a national celebrity, but
...ther priests, Religious, and lay persons
...imilar energy and less recognition.
...*rum*, the encyclical of Pope Leo XIII
...1891 had given Catholics a rationale
...vism. The encyclical had not only up-
...nt to unionize, it had rejected the
laissez-faire economics and urged the
...peratives and other voluntary organi-

I provided another opportunity to get
...her John J. Burke, a Paulist and editor
...orld magazine, was dismayed by the

Fitzgerald turned away from their early Catholicism and reflected little or no religious idealism in their work.

But if Eugene O'Neill cared little for Catholicism, it was equally true that the average Catholic paid little attention to O'Neill's plays. The typical Catholic was a blue-collar worker who didn't go to the theater. He had heroes like Gene Tunney, the heavyweight boxing champion, or Babe Ruth of the Yankees. Ruth was an un-assimilated man, a crude, happy-go-lucky nonconformist who came out of a Xaverian Brothers industrial school in Baltimore to become the most celebrated and colorful player the game of baseball had ever known. He was a figure with which many Catholics could identify.

There was still another sports hero during the 1920s who made Catholic hearts beat with pride. The son of Norwegian immigrants, he was a convert who could have been a successful chemist had he not become a football coach instead. His name was Knute Rockne, and the teams he built at Notre Dame had a special meaning for rank-and-file Catholics who had never been to college themselves and who had a vague contempt for intellectual achievement. They relished the regularity with which Rockne teams beat Michigan, Carnegie Tech, Stanford, and other strongholds of the social elite. It was said that Catholics knew the Four Horsemen better than they knew the four Gospels. There was truth in that.

A Catholic Runs for President

So for the most part Catholics were content in their retreat from the turbulence of the times. They would rather honor athletes than intellectuals. They felt cozy and secure in the faith, happy to be sheltered from the hurricane. There was a certain satisfaction in knowing that their own house was in order, even if the rest of society was not.

If the Roman mentality produced a high degree of conformism among Catholics, at least it gave them a feeling of unity and common purpose. That mentality was being fostered at the highest level now by having the most promising candidates for the priesthood trained at the North American College in Rome. And it reached a ceremonial climax of sorts in 1926 when Chicago was host to the International Eucharistic Congress, drawing high ecclesiastics from all parts of the globe. It was a grand display of piety and triumphalism.

It would be wrong to assume, however, that the sense of separation that Catholics experienced in America during the 1920s was entirely of their own choosing. We have already noted how a resurgence of Nativism kept many doors closed to Catholics. That attitude was not confined to uneducated Americans. There were many sincere, intelligent non-Catholics who still believed Rome had designs on American liberties.

The nation had a chance to test that belief in 1928 when a Catholic, Alfred E. Smith, ran for president.

Al Smith was a four-term governor of New York when he won the Democratic nomination for president. He was a colorful character with little formal education who spoke with a thick New York City accent and smoked cigars. For all his personality traits, his years as governor were marked by honest,

efficient leader
He was opposed
supporter of pu

The nominati
Atlantic Monthl
patriotism of Ca
loyalty to the V
office. Smith r
Father Duffy) i
absolute freedom
ity of all churche
as a matter of ri

While the ans
Monthly, it could
as a result of the
voters all over t
eastern manneris
most of all by his
would never be de
dice gripped larg
weeks went on, S
came the targets o
paign. And whe
November Herber
444 electoral vote

If there was any
lics, it was a confir
ers in America. If
America, then Ca
part of them. Inste
heroes like Babe R
could command
strength. The time

peacemaker an
in the future.

14. A

As we noted
ism in the fir
chilling effect
Original rese
upon as poten
minds in the (
their energies
was social act

Social actio
American Cat
dinal Gibbons
of workingme
had long been
with hundred
homes stretch
J. Flanagan's
had made t
thousands of c
labored with

Rerum No
issued back i
for social act
held the rig
philosophy o
creation of cc
zations.

World Wa
involved. Fa
of *Catholic*

disruption and human suffering caused by the war. In 1917, with the approval of Cardinal Gibbons, he created the National Catholic War Council to mobilize and coordinate Catholic service programs. Aided by other groups, the council was soon operating canteens for servicemen, relief programs for orphans and refugees, and was promoting war-loan drives.

Formation of the National Catholic Welfare Conference

When the war was over Father Burke and some of the bishops felt that the council should be continued. It had proven to be a valuable way of channeling the energies of many dioceses and private agencies toward the solution of common social problems. But Burke's proposal was not greeted with unanimous approval.

Theoretically, under Church law, each bishop is supreme in his own diocese and answerable only to the pope. The law makes no provision for a national secretariat that might infringe on the pope's prerogatives on one hand or a bishop's prerogatives on the other. No other nation had such an organization, and there was a sizeable group of bishops who did not want to see one in the United States either. On the other hand, public issues were becoming too complex to be handled by bishops working independently. Nor would an occasional synod of bishops suffice. So after considerable debate, and with the approval of the Vatican, the bishops in 1919 approved the creation of the National Catholic Welfare Conference with offices in Washington, D.C.

Although it was called a "welfare" conference, the

NCWC actually served as a coordinating agency for many activities that had nothing to do with social work. It quickly became a clearinghouse of information for parochial schools and established policies for the Catholic school system nationally. It established a communications department and set up a news service for diocesan newspapers. It coordinated the activities of lay organizations. It served as the bishops' lobbying agency on Capitol Hill.

The first peacetime task of the NCWC was to alert American Catholics to the evils of socialism. It seems that the bishops shared the fears most Americans had about the Russian revolution. A nationwide civic education program in a dozen languages was undertaken by the new organization. But hand in hand with this the agency was thinking along positive lines to stimulate reconstruction after the war. A few months after it was founded the conference issued a startlingly progressive blueprint for postwar economic life. Among other things it urged the retention of high wartime wages, the recognition of labor unions, profit-sharing in industry, and equal wages for women who do the same work as men.

The controversial report was the work of Father John A. Ryan, a professor at Catholic University who soon moved over to become head of the NCWC social action department. Ryan, like many of his contemporaries, had been inspired by *Rerum Novarum*. But there were American influences at work on him too. The American Church still had its roots deep in the working class. As Cardinal Cushing of Boston observed later, "Every one of our bishops and archbishops is the son of a workingman."

Even with their working-class origins, some Cath-

Catherine de Hueck, center, was one of many social activists who dedicated themselves to racial and economic justice.

The right to unionize was strongly defended by papal teachings and by American Catholic leaders in the 1920s and 1930s.

olics did not like Ryan's program. The president of the National Association of Manufacturers complained that Ryan's ideas smacked of socialism; that was to be expected. But when Ryan began to hear similar reactions from Catholics, a more vigorous response was taken. In 1922 he created the Catholic Congress on Industrial Problems and established Traveling Schools of Social Thought with mass meetings around the country. Not everyone welcomed them. A Catholic employer in Chicago stood up and announced that the Church should stick to saving souls "and not be like Protestant churches butting into everybody's business."

As a matter of fact, it wasn't an opportune moment to be butting into people's business. The postwar economic bloom was in full flower. There were plenty of jobs. Americans were living better than they ever had before. The stock market went up in a dizzying spiral that promised profits for almost anybody who had money to invest. But in 1929 the bottom dropped out and the Great Depression set in with a vengeance.

The Depression had a devastating effect on the way Americans lived and put unprecedented strains on public and private charitable institutions. By July 1932 about twelve million persons were unemployed; more than five thousand banks, mostly rural ones, had failed, erasing the life savings of untold thousands of people; the average monthly wages were only 60% of what they had been three years before. Church agencies did what they could to relieve human suffering, but it was clear that private charity alone could not handle the problem.

At last the time had come for serious consideration of John A. Ryan's social reconstruction program.

Many of the ideas he proposed were reflected in the legislation of President Franklin Roosevelt's New Deal starting in 1933. While it would be hard to prove that the New Deal was actually "inspired" by Catholic activists such as Ryan, it is undoubtedly true that the New Deal benefited from the moral climate they created. Another impetus came from the encyclical *Quadragesimo Anno* of Pope Pius XI which echoed and enlarged on many of the ideas expressed by Pope Leo XIII forty years earlier. Roosevelt quoted approvingly from *Quadragesimo Anno* in his first election campaign. Both Ryan and Msgr. Francis J. Haas, director of the National Catholic School for Social Service, were named to serve on numerous boards and commissions that put the New Deal into effect. Haas also gained renown as a strike mediator during the wave of labor unrest that swept the country in the middle and late 1930s.

Other Social Activists

By now there were labor priests in most large cities, and courses were established to teach the social encyclicals. Three such schools were operated by the Association for Catholic Trade Unionists started by Father John Monaghan in New York City in 1937. Father Daniel Lord of St. Louis enrolled thousands of teenagers in his Summer Schools of Catholic Action.

Out in America's heartland where agricultural purchasing power had dropped by 50% since the Depression started, the National Catholic Rural Life Conference sought to spread the Church's social teachings among farmers and their families. The conference's *1939 Manifesto on Rural Life* won national recognition, and its activities eventually spread to 117 dioceses.

Suddenly it seemed that social justice was a popular cause, until it became positively fashionable to espouse economic reform. A parish priest from Royal Oak, Michigan, named Charles E. Coughlin inserted some comments on the social encyclicals into a radio sermon he was delivering. When the public responded favorably, Coughlin expanded on the subject. His radio talks began to command a large following in many parts of the country extending beyond all denominational lines. He was an early supporter of Roosevelt and the New Deal.

However, Coughlin's crusade soon took a new and disquieting tone. In his attacks on bankers and other wealthy persons, it became clear that he was attacking Jews as a group. Aware of the power he commanded as a radio speaker, he began to use it for his own political ambitions. He organized the National Union for Social Justice, a political alliance that espoused isolationism, inflation and anti-semitism. Eventually, Coughlin was silenced by his bishop and his movement fell apart.

But while Coughlin sought power for himself, many other persons were willing to labor for social justice without any thought of personal gain. One such person was Dorothy Day, a journalist and onetime Communist who in 1932 opened a house of hospitality for the poor in New York City. Day had been inspired by Peter Maurin who was promoting various forms of Christian spirituality strongly influenced by socialism. Together they started publishing the *Catholic Worker*, a penny newspaper that served as a trumpet for their genteel Christian Marxixm. They also established about thirty houses of hospitality in cities around the country.

While it may have seemed fragile at birth, the Catholic Worker Movement proved to be an enduring force in the American Church. Several generations of lay persons and clergy came out of its houses of hospitality ready to serve the poor and to give themselves to the principles of economic justice and personal non-violence. It was partly through the example of Dorothy Day and other Catholic Workers that pacifism came to be accepted as a legitimate alternative for American Catholics.

Another woman who gave herself to the poor during this period was Catherine de Hueck who had been born in Russia and was married to a nobleman. She started settlement houses in Toronto and then in Chicago, Washington, D.C., and New York. Her Friendship House in Harlem sponsored interracial programs and crusaded against segregation. The time he spent at the Harlem center left a lasting impression on young Thomas Merton.

One priest who did more than anyone else to promote the cause of racial understanding was Jesuit John LaFarge. The son of a famous artist with the same name, LaFarge spent fifteen years on the rural missions, which brought him close to the plight of the American Black citizen. Moving to New York City in 1926 to become an editor of the Jesuit magazine *America*, he started the first Catholic Interracial Council. The council idea quickly spread to other cities, and LaFarge lived to be a revered figure among Blacks and Whites, Christians and Jews.

Several bishops also played leading roles in the

movement for economic justice and racial brotherhood. The foremost among them was Bishop Bernard
Sheil of Chicago. He was the originator of the Catholic Youth Organizations that brought sports and social programs to parishes across the country. Sheil
was a tireless public speaker, a friend of labor unions,
interracial groups, and other movements that
worked for slum clearance, desegregation and civil
rights. It was largely through the efforts of people
like Sheil and LaFarge that the anti-semitic barbs of
Father Coughlin were blunted and a new era of understanding between American Jews and Catholics
began.

All of these people—John Burke, John Ryan,
Dorothy Day, John LaFarge, and Bernard Sheil—
helped to instill a new sense of civic responsibility in
American Catholics during the 1920s and 1930s.
They strengthened that side of Catholicism that does
not seek to convert the other but merely to improve
his life and ensure that he receives justice.

In a period when theological speculation was temporarily shelved, progressives and others found an
outlet for their energies in social action. It was the
sort of activity that had a special attraction for Americans, and it was destined to bear a great deal of fruit.

15. Missionary Outreach

There were several benefits to be gained from the
social activism in the American Church prior to
World War II. Besides helping people, the activists
provided living witness to the fact that Catholics—or
at least a significant number of them—were devoting

their lives to Gospel values. The poor were being ministered to and the weak defended. The full weight of the Church was put behind the labor movement. And however much they shunned intellectual achievement, the clergy and the Catholic people lived lives of dedication and self-sacrifice to a degree that would be hard to imagine one or two generations later.

The fact of the matter was that the American Church during the darkest phase of its "ghetto period" was a dynamic and growing community. There was a sense of common loyalty and unity of purpose that bound its members together. Vocations to the priesthood and the religious life were multiplying. Priests and people displayed a high degree of confidence that was reinforced by the assurance that their Church was the "true" one and their pope an infallible teacher.

Self-assurance of this kind inevitably prompts people to share their good fortune with outsiders. For Catholics during this period it gave rise to a vigorous missionary effort at home and overseas.

Missions in the United States

The missionary enterprise was, of course, not a new discovery for Americans. Much of the Church's energy over the years had been given to carrying the Gospel to the far corners of North America, and even the Vatican considered the United States a mission land until 1908.

The bulk of those efforts, however, had been given to serving far-flung groups of Catholics. Proportionately little preaching was aimed at Protestants or the unchurched. True, Isaac Hecker had set out to evangelize Protestants, but he met with little success—and anyway, Anglo-Americans were not much attracted to a Church with such a pronounced immigrant flavor.

By the second decade in the 20th century the immigrant veneer on the Church had begun to wear off. The virtual stoppage of immigration by 1930 accelerated the pace at which the Catholic community was becoming "middle American." By this time, mixed marriages between Catholics and non-Catholics had already begun to result in a significant number of "conversions." The non-Catholic spouse who saw his or her children go to a parochial school (Canon law required that the children be raised as Catholics), listened to their catechism answers, attended their First Communions and Confirmations, was gently but gradually drawn into parish life.

Organized efforts at evangelizing non-Catholics began with the Paulists and the Catholic Missionary Union they founded in 1896. The union's Apostolic Mission House at Catholic University trained several thousand diocesan priests for mission work in their own dioceses. The Catholic Extension Society, founded in 1905, raised funds which eventually paid to construct seven thousand small, rural churches, and sent railroad chapels, and mobile chapels into the hinterlands. These efforts had enough impact by 1928 that voters in the Al Smith campaign told a joke about why Catholics called each other "Mac." According to the punchline, "Mac" stood for "make America Catholic."

But the election of 1928 made it clear to Catholics

just how ignorant rural Americans were about their Church. Folks along the back roads were firmly convinced that Catholics rejected the Bible, that they were plotting to take over the federal government and perhaps bring back the Inquisition. Too much attention had been given by Catholic leaders to the cities, where the Catholic population was concentrated, and not enough to the small towns and villages.

From the 1930s onward, the Paulists, Jesuits, and other religious communities began devoting a larger share of their time to rural missions. Beginning in 1939 the Glenmary Missioners directed their efforts at areas where less than one percent of the population was Catholic. They used tents, trailers, and private homes to educate people about the Catholic Church, and, at the same time, sponsored and assisted rural anti-poverty programs.

The main task of these missionaries was not so much to make converts (which were few), but simply to demonstrate that Catholics are not ogres—that they are decent human beings who sincerely believe in God and respect civil liberties. The real breakthrough in this effort did not come until after World War II when industries from the north began to invade rural America, bringing a good percentage of Catholic laborers along with them. But in the meantime, a great deal of foundation-laying had been done.

The period between the wars also saw a stepped-up program of evangelization of Blacks and other minority groups. The Josephite Fathers, who came from England to the United States in 1871, were most actively engaged in the Black missions. Initially they created separate parishes for their converts in the south, an expediency that proved to be unsatisfactory by the middle of the century. Since then, all parishes and schools have been integrated.

The Blessed Sacrament Sisters of Mother Katherine Drexel also continued their work among Blacks and Indians. In 1925 they founded Xavier University in New Orleans, the first Catholic university for Black students. Along with the Jesuits and other communities, their work among the Indians was so successful that by the time of the bicentennial in 1976 nearly half of all the Indians in the United States were Catholic.

Mainline Catholics were also becoming aware that help was needed by their Spanish-speaking brothers in the southwest. Chicanos and other Latins did not always accept the culture of English-speaking Americans, and, while they clung tenaciously to their Catholic faith, they did not have the money to build up the kind of parish network that had become the American norm. Diocesan priests staffed most of the rural Chicano parishes, aided in part by Franciscans who by now had returned to their old Spanish missions.

It would be wrong to assume from all these examples that Catholics threw all their missionary energies during this time into rural areas. That was far from the case. The cities also drew their share of missionary zeal. In the 1930s the Catholic Evidence Guild started sending young people out to preach Catholicism in city streets and parks. Catholic Information Centers blossomed at storefront locations, and a whole generation of clergy and lay people gave themselves to the heady business of convert-making.

Just as the early Church gloried in tales of martyrdom, American Catholics in the 1930s and 1940s revelled in their own literary form—the convert story. They found it immensely gratifying when famous personalities such as Clare Booth Luce, Heywood Broun, and Knute Rockne made their "submission to Rome." Not a few of the celebrities were instructed in the faith by Msgr. Fulton J. Sheen, a dynamic young theology professor at Catholic University who in time became a celebrated author, television personality, the principal fund-raiser for the missions, and eventually Bishop of Rochester, New York.

All of these efforts brought a steady number of adults into the Church. The number was not large in view of the amount of publicity involved. In 1960, the peak year for conversions, only 146,000 adult Americans became Catholics. Yet the missionary enterprise was important because it was a sign that Catholics in America were losing their defensiveness. For the first time large numbers of them were willing to go into marketplace, confront those who disagreed with them, and confess openly to their religious tradition.

Foreign Missionary Activities

Considering the vast amount of work that had to be done within the borders of the United States, the American Church had little money or manpower to give to the foreign missions prior to 1900. Even seventy years after that some dioceses in the west and southwest, desperately short of priests, were recruiting clergy from Ireland.

Nevertheless, early in the 20th century at least some areas of the United States were sufficiently staffed with priests and could give some attention to the worldwide task of evangelization.

The first training school for foreign missionaries had been established at Techny, Illinois in 1906. But the real impetus did not come for another dozen years, and it was inspired by a priest who had spent a long time in the rural horse-and-buggy apostolate in North Carolina. Initially, Father Thomas Price wanted to create an association of priests to convert the south. When those plans fizzled, he teamed up with Father James A. Walsh of Boston to start a foreign mission society. They bought a hill in New York State overlooking the Hudson River to build their seminary, and called it Maryknoll.

In 1918 the first contingent of Maryknoll priests arrived in China. Price died that year and Walsh assumed leadership of the society. The first years were difficult, but by the time Walsh died in 1936 Maryknoll could claim 200 priests and 500 sisters, most of them in China. Unfortunately, the communist takeover after World War II ended all missionary efforts there. Since then, Maryknollers have become increasingly active in Latin America and Africa.

Other religious communities have also made significant contributions to the mission fields. The Divine Word Fathers, operating out of their Techny, Illinois base, have sent hundreds of priests to the South Pacific. Between the two World Wars the American Jesuits also became involved in mission work, to a point where they eventually were the largest Catholic mission force. By the 1950s, there were nearly one thousand American Jesuits serving abroad—mainly in India, the Philippines, Japan, Taiwan, and Central America.

In addition to sending people overseas, American Catholics eventually sent a great deal of money. By 1919 they were contributing a million dollars a year to the foreign missions. Since then, under the urging of the American Society for the Propagation of the Faith, that figure has been multiplied many times over.

With the desolation brought on by World War II, a new element was added to the missionary outreach. Clearly, Americans had an obligation to care for the needy out of their abundance, and the Catholic Church, being international in its organization, offered a convenient distribution channel. Catholic Relief Services, founded in 1943 to help European refugees, grew to become the largest private relief agency in the world—larger than CARE, and second in size only to the United States government aid program. It continues to distribute tons of food and clothes to needy persons and disaster victims in all corners of the world.

In a similar manner, the Catholic Near East Welfare Association has been a channel for the distribution of food and clothing to people in the Near East, including Palestinian refugees; and the Catholic Medical Mission Bureau sends drugs and medical equipment, donated or bought at cost, to mission stations all over the globe.

Looking back, one can say that the missionary phase of American Catholicism helped to free it from the stay-at-home mentality that had gripped the Church since the beginning of the century. Not only

Street preaching, left, was one part of the "convert apostolate." Gradually such preachers were replaced by mid-city information centers.

Below, Thomas Price, left, and James A. Walsh, center, pose with their first group of Maryknoll missionaries.

did it bring the message of the Gospel to outsiders, it tended to release Catholics themselves from a narrow-minded mentality, giving them an appreciation of lives different from their own, and proved to be a beneficial experience for both the givers and the takers.

VI
The Renewal of
Catholicism

16. The Ghetto Collapses

During the 1960s the walled city that symbolized the experience of Catholic life in America collapsed, probably forever, under pressures that grew from inside and from without. The metaphor applies both to the Catholic mentality and to the way Catholics actually lived their lives. The lifestyle of most Catholics was beginning to change, and with the new lifestyle came a change in the way they thought about things.

Sociological Pressures

To start with, the vast majority of Catholics had always made their homes in cities. A survey made in the 1950s showed that, although the Catholic Church was the largest single religious body in the nation, it ranked thirty-third out of thirty-eight in rural membership. Catholicism was an urban phenomenon. Immigrants who flocked here in the 19th century were encouraged to remain in the cities where their Church could protect them against Protestant influences. There they worked in the factories, joined unions, entered into politics.

In the aftermath of World War II the pattern of Catholic life began to change. Guaranteed a free college education by the G.I. Bill of Rights, the sons of immigrants could aspire to better jobs and homes in the suburbs. Having seen France, Italy, or the South Pacific during the war, they felt less attachment to the narrow limits of their urban neighborhood. At the same time, less affluent jobhunters from the south and the Caribbean began flocking to the big cities in search of employment, thus changing the character of the inner-city. The high-water mark of ethnic Catholicism had been passed.

Out in the suburbs, people were less likely to be bound together by church affiliation. Economic instead of religious considerations determined the quality of life and the pattern of neighborhoods. Instead of parish socials, people were likely to congregate at backyard barbecues or Little League games where it mattered little whether one was a Catholic, Protestant, or Jew. And with the help of automobiles and the general postwar affluence, the population became more mobile, less attached to any one community or style of life.

Religion is, to a large extent, a "way of living." It is a style of life that has its own patterns and rhythms, rising and falling with the seasons of the liturgical year and with each passing generation of believers. Because of the rapid economic and social changes that followed World War II, the familiar equilibrium of Catholic life became shaky. Old values seemed to lose their force when applied to a technological and non-religious society.

Gradually, almost without knowing it, Catholics began to drift into what has been called the American "civil religion"—a vague, generalized belief in the rightness of the American nation, the propriety of wealth and hard work, and a certain wariness with hard-line orthodoxy. Like their unchurched neighbors, Catholics became pragmatists: what "works" is "good," what doesn't "work" is "pointless." The kind of assimilation that some churchmen had been warning about for more than a century was at last occurring within the Catholic population; Catholics, like everyone else, were becoming "secularists." For a growing number of them religion came to be seen as an activity suitable for Sunday mornings, with no relevance for the rest of the week. Catholic leaders discovered that their power to influence public policy or private behavior was shrinking.

The Institution at Its Zenith

But first, before the impact of all these forces could really be felt, the Catholic Church in America achieved its zenith of influence and institutional power. The "baby boom" of the 1940s and 1950s added immensely to its strength. In 1945, when the war ended, there were twenty-four million Catholics in the United States. By 1960 that figure had climbed to forty million. Thousands of young men, disillusioned with war and eager to create a healthier postwar world, entered seminaries or monasteries. When the war ended the nation had thirty-eight thousand priests. By 1969 there were fifty-three thousand.

Catholic education was booming. In 1945 approximately two and a half million children attended parochial schools. Fifteen years later the number had nearly doubled. Classrooms were jammed with youngsters (sometimes as many as seventy to a room), and Church authorities instituted major building programs to keep up with the demand. The New York archdiocese kicked off a twenty-five million dollar fund-raising drive in 1947. Other dioceses followed suit, especially on the west coast where millions of easterners were flooding into the cities of Los Angeles, San Francisco, and San Diego.

As the number of Catholics grew, so did their influence on politics and national affairs. There was still a residue of Nativism in the country (evident when Congress would not let President Harry S. Truman appoint an ambassador to the Vatican), but its influence was diminishing. During this period the United States was caught up in the coldest days of its Cold War with the Soviet Union—a struggle in which the Vatican, too, had much at stake and in which millions of American Catholics, second or third-generation immigrants from eastern Europe, were ardent participants. The FBI and other intelligence agencies were able to recruit a whole generation of agents from Catholic college graduates, knowing that their loyalty and anti-communist fervor were beyond question.

No one was more enthusiastic about anti-communism than Senator Joseph McCarthy who pitched his campagin on the fear of communist infiltration of the American government. His well-publicized attacks on prominent persons received widespread support among Catholics, both clergy and lay, even though a significant portion of Catholic

Senator Joseph McCarthy, left, capitalized on fears of communist influences during the 1950s. John F. Kennedy, right, typified a new breed of Catholic who felt fully integrated in American life.

The Second Vatican Council had an especially strong impact on American Catholicism, which was out of touch with liberalizing influences in Europe.

opinion (rallying around *Commonweal* and *America* magazines) opposed him. But whether friends or foes, most Catholics received some measure of satisfaction in watching McCarthy grilling those members of the ruling elite who only a generation before had been calling Catholics unpatriotic.

The climate of religious toleration in America was slowly changing, bringing more Catholics into government and public life. Although only fourteen Catholics had been appointed to cabinet positions between 1789 and 1955, ten of those fourteen received appointments after 1933. Also, by 1955 there were ten Catholics serving in the United States Senate and seventy-two in the House of Representatives. A dozen years later the number had increased once more—fourteen Catholics were in the Senate and ninety-four were members in the House, making Catholics the largest single denomination in Congress.

Perhaps surprisingly to those who had warned about such an eventuality, a single "Catholic bloc" failed to emerge from this representation. As always, legislators tended to disagree with one another, and a Catholic legislator found that he (or she) could disagree with a fellow-Catholic just as easily as with a non-Catholic. On matters of Church discipline or doctrine, however, there was no disagreement: all Catholics spoke with one voice, and that voice was the voice of the Church expressed through the statements of the bishops, and ultimately of the pope. Still feeling the aftershocks of the Americanism and Modernism "heresies," American Catholics were inordinately sensitive to doctrinal deviation. Yet their religious unity, while making them strong and purposeful, had the other effect of blinding them to new needs and new lines of inquiry.

In Europe at this time the Church was beginning to reconsider issues that had led to the Modernism crisis fifty years earlier. Pope Pius XII encouraged developments in liturgy and Scripture study while closing the door to some other lines of study that he felt were too threatening. Some intellectual leaders, like the Jesuit scientist Teilhard de Chardin, were commanded to keep silent about their undoctrinaire ideas. Yet despite the Vatican's caution European theology was developing ideas that would astonish the Americans who went to Rome for the first session of Vatican Council II.

Even in America there were some signs of change. In the 1940s Jesuit theologian John Courtney Murray began publishing a series of articles which proposed that the American system of Church-State separation was compatible with traditional Catholic teaching. It was not a new idea; Archbishop Ireland had said much the same thing a half-century earlier, and Vatican II would later endorse it. But by 1955 some churchmen had become alarmed by Murray's thesis. At last he was ordered to stop writing on the subject.

Just the previous year, Msgr. John Tracy Ellis, a Church historian at Catholic University in Washington, D.C. charged in effect that American Catholicism had become an intellectual wasteland. Pointing to the lack of achievement by graduates of Catholic colleges and universities, he maintained that the Church had failed to produce intellectual leaders and, indeed, was not programmed to do so. The debate that Ellis started continued through the

1950s and led to other, more pointed, questions: Doesn't intellectual attainment require academic freedom? And how can the Church produce leaders when it simply will not allow scholars to discuss some issues? Thus the stage was set in the United States for the opening of Vatican Council II.

A Pope, A President, A Council

The council that was called by Pope John XXIII did not disrupt the Church as much as it gave vent to those pressures that were already building up within the institution. The pope himself was a friendly, paternal figure whose democratic instincts appealed to Americans accustomed to the more austere manners of his predecessor, Pius XII. Pope John described the function of the council as *aggiornamento* (updating), with special emphasis on internal reform and Christian unity.

On both sides of the Atlantic Catholic scholars already had been meeting privately with Protestant counterparts to discuss their different traditions and study ways of bringing their Churches closer. In the United States a great deal of groundwork had been done by Jesuit Gustave Weigel, a colleague of John Courtney Murray's. Through the efforts of Weigel and others, a significant new climate of religious understanding was being generated among Church leaders. How strongly those feelings were shared by rank-and-file Church members was about to be put to a test.

The test came in November of 1960. John F. Kennedy, a senator from Massachusetts and a Roman

Catholic, was campaigning for the presidency. Remembering how Alfred E. Smith was overwhelmed thirty years earlier, some observers felt that Kennedy's religion would prove to be an insurmountable barrier to election. Indeed, the "religious issue" emerged early in the campaign, and Kennedy (unlike Smith) met it head-on with clear assertions that his religion would not impede his functioning as president. To the "bible belt" voters in West Virginia he "swore on the bible" that he would not put his Church before his country, and to representatives of the Houston Ministerial Association he stated: "I do not accept the right of any ecclesiastical official to tell me what to do in the sphere of my public responsibility as an elected official." Kennedy won the West Virginia primary, and in the end he also won the presidential election—but by such a small margin that it was impossible to tell whether his religion had aided him (in Catholic precincts) or held him back.

Regardless of the closeness of the victory, the fact that Kennedy won was recognized on all sides as a clear sign that Catholics were now full members of American society. Nativism was finally put to rest. The young president's conduct in office vastly increased his popular support, and when he was killed, when his body was carried from St. Matthew's Cathedral and buried in Arlington National Cemetery, the Church, the State, and the people were united in mourning.

Before that sad day, however, the bishops had twice gone to Rome for sessions of Pope John's council. The initial American response to the great religious gathering was positive, but many Catholics were struck with bewilderment when the debates started.

Where had all these new theological ideas come from? The American bishops, clergy, and laity buckled down to the task of reeducation. Theological notions once considered dangerous were now in vogue. John Courtney Murray was taken out of limbo in the United States and rushed to Rome to serve as an "expert." Theological journals flourished. Newsmen—both for the daily press and for diocesan newspapers—had to develop new skills to report on the struggles that took place in the council. European theologians such as Karl Rahner and Hans Küng visited the United States to lecture before admiring audiences of Catholics and Protestants. It was a time of unparalleled excitement and ferment.

Much of what the council did had an appeal to Americans. The decree on the liturgy—the first text approved—laid the groundwork for a system of worship that was less rigid and more familiar. The notion of collegiality contained in the decree on the Church pointed to more democratic structures among the hierarchy and between the clergy and the people. Ultimately it would give rise to parish and diocesan councils and to national councils of bishops patterned after America's National Catholic Welfare Conference (now rechristened the United States Catholic Conference).

The Constitution on the Church in the Modern World supplied a *carte blanche* to the kind of social activism that had inspired several generations of Americans. The decree on ecumenism was based on the spirit of toleration that had been accepted as an American ideal since the time of the Bill of Rights. Finally, and most significantly for Americans, the council gave its endorsement to the principles of re-

ligious liberty and the separation of Church and
State which were nurtured so carefully in North
America. It might even be said that the Declaration
on Religious Freedom was America's gift to the Catholic Church.

The euphoria of the council, of course, could not last
forever. As conservatives had long predicted, once
some parts of the Catholic "package" were changed,
all the other parts would at least be open to question.
In practice, the delicate balance between change and
continuity, between preserving the essentials of faith
and reforming its cultural unessentials, was difficult
to maintain. It seemed to many believers that the
faith was in disarray. Where a few years previously
they could ask themselves "What does the Church
believe?" they now had to ask "What do I believe?" It
was a painful adjustment. For some it resulted in a
loss of faith. For others—including many seminarians, priests, and Religious—it involved leaving the
religious life to take up different lifestyles appropri-
ate to their new self-understanding. Some bishops
and priests had trouble adjusting to a style of leadership in which they had to share responsibility with
those above and below them. Lay people were con-
fused and upset. They winced when they saw pictures
of priests and especially sisters on picket lines or
using their new freedom of involvement in social
issues. Some people became part of a conservative
backlash that blamed the council for all the problems
of the Church.

All these developments pointed to one undeniable
fact: the American Catholic Church was no longer the
tightly organized monolith it once was made out to
be. Catholics were owning up to the fact that they

were divided from each other on many religious and secular issues. No one could know where the course of history was leading. The ghetto walls were gone. American Catholics were face-to-face with the opportunities and dangers of modern life.

17. The Changing Parish

The 1960s were a time of great upheaval in the American Catholic Church. On one hand Catholics experienced a new sense of freedom in the civil society; young people could even dream of growing up to be president. But if it was suddenly easier to be a full partner in America, it seemed more difficult to be a Catholic. Somehow, in the process of renewal, the sense of community that held Catholics together for more than a century had been weakened. It was almost as if, having achieved full integration into American society, they no longer needed the smaller communities in which they had been raised.

The Role of Parishes in American Catholicism

We have already had some indication of the important role that parish life played in the development of the American Church. The Catholic parish provided a comfortable haven for immigrants who still felt ill at ease in their New World surroundings. It offered material welfare, education, entertainment, leadership, opportunities for service, and of course worship. Here they could speak their own languages, honor their Old World saints, and preserve ethnic skills such as dancing, cooking, and needlework.

Those urban American parishes were large by European standards. Because immigrants tended to settle in separate neighborhoods, their parishes took on various ethnic colorings—Italian, German, Polish, or Slovakian. Separate parishes (and in time, separate dioceses) were created for Eastern Rite Catholics who were in communion with Rome. (Statistics in 1977 show more than 600,000 Eastern Rite Catholics in the United States organized in six Exarchates [dioceses] and numerous independent parishes. They included Ukranians, Greeks, Melchites, Maronites, Armenians, Romanians, Byelorussians, Chaldeans, and Russians.) The very size of the parishes provided ample room for the variety of services the parishes provided, and also served to gratify ethnic pride. On Sundays the immense buildings were packed with worshipers who knelt or stood silently to witness the ornate liturgies. Those who took part in the service had the intense feeling of belonging to a community that was larger and more important than themselves; they did not have to do anything, they simply had to belong.

In later years it became fashionable to describe those large parishes as "factories" that dispensed wisdom and blessings on an assembly line. It is true that the communities were generally too large to give attention to each individual member, but it would be untrue to imply that Catholics in that era were shallow or lacking in piety. The early 20th century was a period of great personal devotion; the churches were beehives of pious activities: novenas, public rosaries, Marian devotions in May and October, benedictions, stations of the cross during Lent, outdoor processions during the summer, and Forty Hours once a year. Ever since 1905 when Pope Pius X had urged frequent reception of Communion, Catholics had trooped to the altar rail in ever-growing numbers. The Holy Name Society and the Women's Altar Guild each had their "Communion Sundays" when members would receive together.

During these high-water years before the council, people gave great attention to the outward display of religion. Youngsters in parochial schools were encouraged to make the sign of the cross every time they passed a Catholic church. The clothing of religious women and priests signified the permanence (and sometimes the rigidity) of their vocations. Fasting and Friday abstinence from meat were strictly enforced, and so was attendance at Mass on holy days. And yet, despite the sincerity of these practices, they sometimes degenerated into automatic responses. The ideal held up for emulation was one of group obedience and conformity instead of personal initiative.

The first changes in this attitude began in the 1920s when the liturgical movement began to promote more authentic and ancient rituals in place of the pious practices that had grown up in the post-Reformation Church. Begun in Europe, the liturgical reform leaped directly to America's midwest where some religious orders (such as the Benedictines) had direct ties to Germany and France and where Catholic life was more in tune with the natural rhythm of the seasons. In 1925 a Benedictine priest named Virgil Michael, just returned from Belgium, started a magazine called *Orate Fratres* at his home monastery of St. John's in Collegeville, Minnesota. Later the

Older parishes tended to be large and impersonal, with few contacts between pastors and individual parishioners.

The charismatic movement, which began in the Catholic Church in 1966, may have signalled the end of the unease generated by Church renewal and a return to more doctrinal, prayerful religion.

Vatican II heightened the desire for a more intimate, personal religious experience like this home Mass.

magazine was renamed *Worship*.

For many years the liturgical movement grew slowly. It gathered momentum in 1947 when an encyclical of Pius XII brought it to the attention of rank-and-file Catholics. In America, after the war, it was promoted vigorously by the privately-founded Liturgical Conference and its series of liturgical weeks that increased in spectacle right through the years of Vatican II.

Despite these years of preparation, the reforms that were promulgated by the council took most American Catholics by surprise. They hadn't expected them. Catholics had long been told that the Mass was an unchanging sacrifice, that Latin was essential to the ritual, and that all externals were necessary for a people bent on maintaining their identity in a hostile world. And even those people who had campaigned vigorously for the reforms were brought up short by the reality of them. By breaking the mold of the Roman ritual the council unintentionally opened the door to different tastes and different needs. People began to improvise. The old church buildings designed for magnificent public liturgies were usually not suitable for the new styles of worship; altars were turned around, choirs rearranged, pews torn out, lecterns added, carpets laid down. A few Catholics sought out smaller meeting places in homes and apartments where they composed their own prayers, sang their own songs. The press began to print stories about the "underground church." There was a growing feeling among some Catholics that parish life was outdated as a center for Christian life.

Added to these changes were the sociological pressures of the postwar period, pressures we discussed in the previous section. The 1950s and 1960s witnessed a dramatic restructuring of urban neighborhoods. White, ethnic Catholics gravitated toward the suburbs where living was more informal and where their parishes had a less significant role in establishing neighborhood patterns. The large church structures left behind in the cities became hollow shells in the midst of decaying neighborhoods. Many of them were torn down.

Those Catholics who remained in the cities were caught up in racial tensions, declining services, high taxation, and urban decay and blight. With a sadness that sometimes boiled up into hostility they watched their old neighborhoods fall apart. A new wave of Nativism swept through American cities; this time the White ethnics, once the targets of Nativism, lined up against Blacks, Latins, and other minority groups. Blue-collar Catholics were infuriated to see some of their own priests and sisters demonstrating on behalf of the underdogs. It seemed to many of them that their Church was betraying them.

Finally, the parish absorbed an additional blow in the decline of the parochial school system. Out in the suburbs where Catholics were fully integrated with their Protestant and Jewish neighbors parents felt little urgency to give their children a Catholic education. In the cities the half-empty parishes, populated largely by older people, could no longer afford the schools. And so the parochial school system which was once the binding force of parish life in the United States began to crumble. There was a diminishing number of religious brothers and sisters who once made up a vast reservoir of low-salaried teachers.

From a shortage of classrooms during the "baby boom," many schools now faced a shortage of pupils. The schools were closed by the hundreds.

The Parish in Evolution

In an effort to deal with these various problems, both religious and social, Catholic parishes in the United States began to evolve new structures and new ministries. Whether they could resurrect the intense parish life typical of preconciliar times was doubtful, but it was clear that some kind of religious community was going to survive.

Consider education. With many parochial schools being phased out, large parishes turned to catechetical centers offering evening or weekend courses to children and adults. By the latter half of the 1970s, almost half of the nation's 18,000 parishes employed full-time professional catechists who ran CCD programs, usually with the help of lay volunteers.

Like those catechists, an increasing number of lay persons began to discover that they could have ministerial roles in the Church. No longer passive pew-holders, they became teachers and lectors, counselors, liturgists, and parish social workers. The permanent deaconate was re-instituted as an official ministry of the Church, and it was extended to married men. Other Catholics, both men and women, became extraordinary ministers of the Eucharist distributing Communion to people in church and to others in hospitals and at home. While the old forms of pastors and curates remained, many dioceses started experiments in team ministry with several priests, or priests and sisters (and sometimes even lay people) sharing a pastorate.

These experiments were spurred on by the principle of collegiality spelled out by Vatican II. Henceforth the Church would be less dictatorial in its government. Just as the bishops formed a "college" with the pope, supporting him and sharing in his teaching function, so the clergy of a diocese formed a "college" with their bishop—and the laity of a parish did the same with their pastor. In the years after Vatican II local communities began to form parish councils to assist in the operation and apostolic works of parishes. A whole generation of bishops, priests, Religious, and lay people had to learn the techniques and the headaches of shared authority.

For many Catholics the emphasis on the mechanics of renewal produced a sense of emptiness and powerlessness. A great deal that had been familiar to them had disappeared; they were no longer at ease with their religious forms, and they yearned for secure surroundings where they could be comfortable and comforted. The feeling, while certainly easy to understand, was not an easy one to satisfy. The era of certainty within the Church was gone. And it seemed that Catholic life, instead of being one substantial meal for all people, was more like a buffet where people could pick and choose a kind of membership that was most suitable to their own temperaments.

One movement that helped many Catholics to focus on the essentials of their faith was the Catholic charismatic renewal which grew in a decade from a handful of graduates in Pittsburgh in 1967 to a point when it conducted a national conference for 33,000 people at Notre Dame. Drawing inspiration from the

pentecostal branches of Protestantism, the movement stressed a return to New Testament Chris-
tianity when believers were said to have special gifts
or "charisms." It encouraged spontaneous prayer instead of rote formulas, and it was effective in creating
tightly-knit local communities.

All of these ministries and movements helped to
underscore the fact that the highly-structured and
centralized parish was a thing of the past. Just what
form the new parish might take was still unclear. It
seemed probable however that the parish
structure—in some form—would continue to exist.
As long as people shared a heritage, there would be a
need to come together and celebrate it. American
Catholics had apparently decided that they didn't
want to live in the past. But that didn't mean they
were entirely willing to let go of it.

18. Yesterday and Tomorrow

As the United States celebrated its 200th birthday,
its Catholic members found themselves still search-
ing for a means to be true to their heritage as believers and as citizens. These were old questions—they
had been asked in the age of John Carroll, they had
been asked during the "Americanism" crisis of the
late 19th century, and they would probably be asked
as long as the Church and State continued to exist.
Yet they were real questions: How can a person be
true to religious faith and political goals at the same
time? And how can any body of people—whether a
civil or religious body—reaffirm old values without
retreating into the past?

The 1960s and 1970s had changed a lot of things. The Vietnam War had undermined America's sense of power, and Watergate its sense of moral superiority. For Catholics, the Vatican Council's so-called "updating" seemed to go beyond that. It struck at the very roots of their commitment.

Rediscovering Ethnicity

There was no doubt about it, the Catholic community was changing. In the old days Catholics had been held together by the sense of being outsiders in America. Nearly all of them were immigrants, largely uneducated, poor, and the targets of persecution. The knowledge that they were underdogs gave Catholics cohesiveness and determination to succeed. But by the 1970s success had largely been won. Surveys in that decade revealed that Catholics were among the more affluent population subgroups in America, and Irish Catholics the most affluent.

But in the process of achieving success, the strong tie between ethnicity and religion was beginning to break down. The current of secularization, discussed earlier, was taking its toll. It no longer followed that because someone was Irish, or Italian, or Polish, that that person was necessarily Catholic. To an increasing extent people were coming to feel that religion was not something they inherit (as ethnicity is) but something they choose. And what's more, they could also choose the manner and style of their membership—whether liberal or conservative, or an occasional Catholic, or charismatic, or social activist, etc. Suddenly there were many *ways* of being Catholic.

On the other hand, although the connection between ethnicity and religion suffered erosion, there was a corresponding revival of interest in ethnicity itself. No longer defensive about their immigrant roots, many citizens began to examine and appreciate their old-world culture more intensely. They were inspired in part by the Black-is-beautiful movement among American negroes and by the incursion of Blacks into the tightly-knit ethnic communities remaining in some big cities (causing not a little racial turmoil). The White ethnics were also moved by feelings of nostalgia for the lost ghetto neighborhoods of their youth, replaced now by the plastic anonymity of suburbia. They became aware that even if the neighborhood was lost, the culture that once existed there could still be valued, preserved, and passed on to another generation. One could still be an American and an ethnic simultaneously, for, as Andrew Greeley wrote, "being a Slovak American (for example) is a way of being an American—a way of dealing yourself into society instead of cutting yourself off from it."

The "melting pot" theory which proposed that all Americans be absorbed into a common culture was at last totally discredited. It probably was never true anyway. Instead Americans tended to celebrate their uniqueness, their variety of skills and cultures, their strengths and differences.

To an increasing extent, the Catholic Church attempted to reflect the diversity of its membership. Its hierarchy represented a cross-section of ethnic cultures that included Cardinal John Krol of Philadelphia (a Polish-American) and Archbishop Robert Sanchez of Santa Fe (a Mexican-American). The Latins migrating from the Caribbean into the eastern cities and the Chicanos in the southwest now made up nearly one-quarter of all U.S. Catholics. At least one-half of the Catholic populations of the New York and Brooklyn dioceses were Hispanic.

The Church also felt the impact from the efforts of Black Americans, who hadn't shared the economic benefits of the postwar boom, to achieve equal rights and opportunities. Individual Catholics and Church agencies mostly supported the civil rights movement of the 1960s. Now nearly one million strong Black Catholics formed a national office to demand aid and a voice in the hierarchy.

Despite the fact that Catholics represented a newly affluent class, their Church had not forgotten its historical commitment to poor and oppressed peoples. For example it mustered widespread support for the plight of migrant farmworkers in the west and southwest (most of them Chicanos), just as it had supported labor unions in the previous century.

In the early 1970s the bishops raised nearly $35,000,000.00 to fund the Campaign for Human Development, a program to help poverty-stricken groups of many races and religions to organize self-help programs.

Human development and hunger on a world scale were thornier problems. Influenced by their trips to Rome where they came into contact with bishops from developing nations, the American bishops were beginning to raise their voices in favor of world economic justice. But there was little indication that the average American Catholic—so newly arrived at affluence—shared their concern.

Vietnam and the Abortion Issue

For all these changes, there were two events which, more than any others, helped to reshape the relationship between the Catholic Church and the American State: the Vietnam War and the abortion issue. We'll look at Vietnam first.

The years after World War II saw the Catholic Church become a stubborn foe of communism. The persecution it suffered in Eastern Europe and China reinforced these feelings—to the point where the Church quite naturally endorsed the American position in the Cold War. When that war heated up in Korea and later in Vietnam, American Catholic leaders and laity tended to equate Catholic policy with American policy. Cardinal Francis Spellman of New York was an outspoken proponent of United States military might, making frequent trips to war zones to bless American soldiers and, by extension, the policies they represented.

But even as the Vietnam War was gaining momentum, hard-line attitudes were softening elsewhere in the Church. The Vatican was making overtures to the communist governments of Eastern Europe in order to reach a level of detente. An increasing number of radical and progressive Catholics began to look disapprovingly on capitalism; for them the socialist governments of Cuba or even China were closer to the values of the Gospel. By the time the bishops met for Vatican II there was a sizeable bloc of prelates opposed to the arms race and in favor of some kind of pacifism. The council endorsed the right of citizens to be conscientious objectors in wartime.

Gradually the mood began to change in the United States as well. A growing number of young Catholics claimed to be pacifists and argued that their religious belief supported it. Draft boards accepted their claims. The statements of the American bishops began to include criticism of the government, and finally opposition to the war. Yet it was still a shock when Fathers Philip and Daniel Berrigan raided a draft board in Catonsville, Maryland where they burned official files as an act of protest. Both men were eventually jailed. Many Catholics were scandalized.

Vietnam was a moral dilemma not just for Catholics but for all Americans. The dissension it caused, the lives it consumed, and its sad conclusion disrupted the nation for a decade and left lasting scars. The abortion issue, while less dramatic, was felt more keenly among Catholics than by other citizens.

In 1973 the United States Supreme Court held in effect that abortion was a legal and permissible medical procedure in all but the last three months of pregnancy. Not only was this ruling in direct conflict with the traditional Catholic teaching that abortion—any abortion—was tantamount to murder, it was also regarded as a kind of betrayal by many conservative Catholics who had stayed with their government on the Vietnam issue. It was clear to them now, as never before, that the policies of the government could not be equated with the policies of the Church.

So for a growing number of Catholics the Vietnam

War, the abortion issue, and a subsequent Supreme Court decision denying federal aid to parochial schools were all signs calling the Church back to a rediscovery of its own separateness.

The Future

Just how that separateness would be worked out, however, was not at all clear. There were large segments of the Catholic population that did not share their leaders' concern with Vietnam or abortion. Public opinion polls revealed that Catholic lay people were no longer docile followers on key moral issues; bishops and clergy would have to compete for the loyalty of the laity, not demand it. That fact was evident from the controversy that followed the encyclical by Pope Paul VI on birth control; the Church had not seen this kind of headlines since the 1890s.

Yet American Catholics sensed as never before the need to think through a host of questions and reach—without bitterness or mistrust—a consensus on key issues. These issues would necessarily include the future of parochial schools and Catholic education in general, the continuing protection of human life and dignity, the equitable sharing of the world's resources, the promotion of personal and political freedom, and, finally, the Christian mandate to bring the Gospel to spiritually starved people.

Challenges of this sort are complex and not easily solved. But the fact that they are difficult does not mean that they are insoluble, any more than it means that people are powerless just because they are not all-powerful. This belief was best expressed nearly two hundred years ago by Alexis de Tocqueville, the Frenchman, who commented so perceptively on America:

> There are those who claim that men are not their own masters here below, but necessarily obey . . . some influential and irresistible forces arising from events. These are false and cowardly doctrines which can never create anything but feeble men and craven nations. Providence did not create man either entirely free or completely in servitude. It traced around every man a fatal circle which he cannot leave. But within that vast confine, men are powerful and free, and so are nations.

The American Catholic Church has had its own "fatal circle" that has hemmed it in, but it has shown itself to be adaptable and sometimes even creative within its boundaries.

In every period of history the Church has interacted with its culture, changing that culture and being changed by it. The Catholic Church has learned from its American experience. Catholics have learned in America how to cherish religious freedom, and they have brought that lesson to the Church as a whole.

But American liberty did more than simply free Catholics from interference. It gave them freedom to live out their faith and give witness to it. Their search as Americans and Catholics for renewed faith and deeper meaning in life can serve to light the way for

The 1970s saw the emergence of a new sensitivity for the welfare of minority peoples. One catalyst for this change was Cesar Chavez, right.

As one result of the Supreme Court decision that legalized some forms of abortion, Catholics began to reevaluate the kind of uncritical approval they had lavished on government policies in the past.

many of their fellow countrymen engaged in the same quest. If the freedom of the American experience has touched the Church, perhaps the rich Gospel heritage of the Church can help to renew and reshape the American dream.

Index

151